LIFE

LIGHT

MAMMAL

MANET

MATTER

MEDIA & COMMUNICATION

MEDIEVAL LIFE

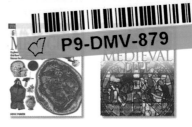

MONET

MONEY

MUMMY

MUSIC

MYTHOLOGY

NORTH AMERICAN INDIAN

OCEAN

OLYMPICS

PERSPECTIVE

PIRATE

PLANT

POND & RIVER

PREHISTORIC LIFE

PRESIDENTS

PYRAMID

RELIGION

RENAISSANCE

REPTILE

RESCUE

ROBOT

ROCKS & MINERALS

RUSSIA

SEASHORE

SHAKESPEARE

SHARK

SHELL

SHIPWRECK

SKELETON

SOCCER

SPACE EXPLORATION

SPORTS

SPY

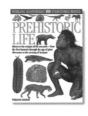

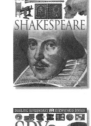

SUBMARINE

SUPER BOWL

TECHNOLOGY

TEXAS

TIME & SPACE

TITANIC

TRAIN

TREE

UNIVERSE

VAN GOGH

VIKING

VOLCANO & EARTHQUAKE

WATERCOLOR

WEATHER

WHALE

WILD WEST

WITCHES & MAGIC-MAKERS

WORLD WAR I

WORLD WAR II

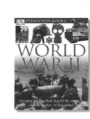

To Johnny,
  Good luck in 4th Grade!
    love Nanny

Sept. '04

Eyewitness
SEASHORE

Sugar kelp

Bladder wrack

Dog whelk

Dogfish eggcases
containing embryos

Carrageen

Hebrew cone shells

Dulse

Common cormorant

Rock oyster

Eyewitness
SEASHORE

Written by
STEVE PARKER

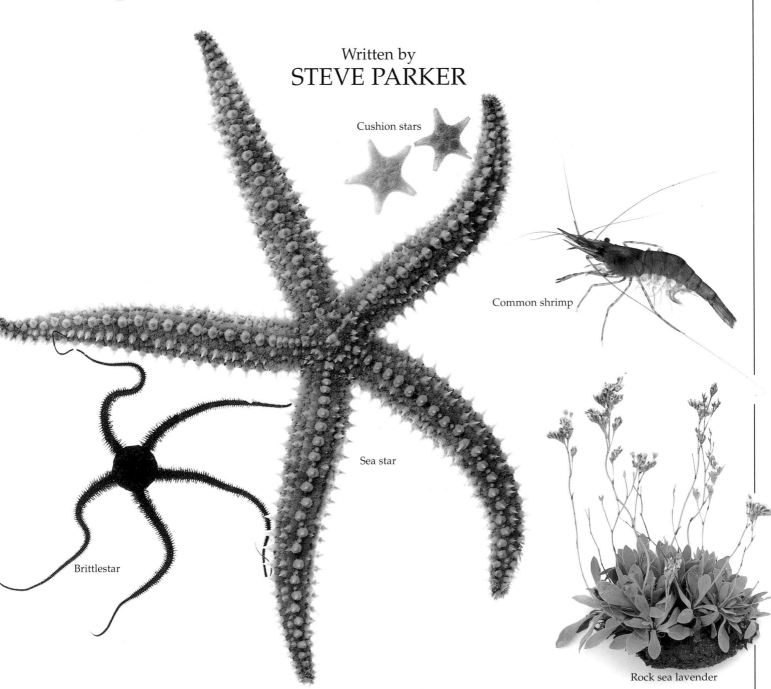

Cushion stars

Common shrimp

Sea star

Brittlestar

Rock sea lavender

DK Publishing, Inc.

Guillemot eggs

Dried seaweed

Pinecone

DK

LONDON, NEW YORK, MELBOURNE,
MUNICH, and DELHI

Project editor Elizabeth Eyres
Art editor Miranda Kennedy
Senior editor Sophie Mitchell
Managing editor Sue Unstead
Managing art editor Roger Priddy
Special photography Dave King
Editorial consultants
The staff of the
Natural History Museum, London

REVISED EDITION
Managing editor Andrew Macintyre
Managing art editor Jane Thomas
Senior editor Kitty Blount
Senior art editor Martin Wilson
Editor Karen O'Brien
Art Editor Ann Cannings
Production Jenny Jacoby
Picture research Lorna Ainger
DTP designer Siu Yin Ho

U.S. editor Elizabeth Hester
Senior editor Beth Sutinis
Art director Dirk Kaufman
U.S. production Chris Avgherinos
U.S. DTP designer Milos Orlovic

Snakelocks anemone

This Eyewitness ® Guide has been conceived by
Dorling Kindersley Limited and Editions Gallimard

This edition published in the United States in 2004
by DK Publishing, Inc., 375 Hudson Street, New York, New York 10014

04 05 06 07 08 10 9 8 7 6 5 4 3 2 1

Copyright © 1989, 2004 Dorling Kindersley Limited

A catalog record for this book is available from the Library of Congress.

ISBN 0-7566-0721-3 (HC) 0-7566-0720-5 (Library Binding)

Color reproduction by Colourscan, Singapore
Printed in China by Toppan Printing Co. (Shenzhen), Ltd.

Gull feathers

Limpet

Pipefish

Discover more at

www.dk.com

Contents

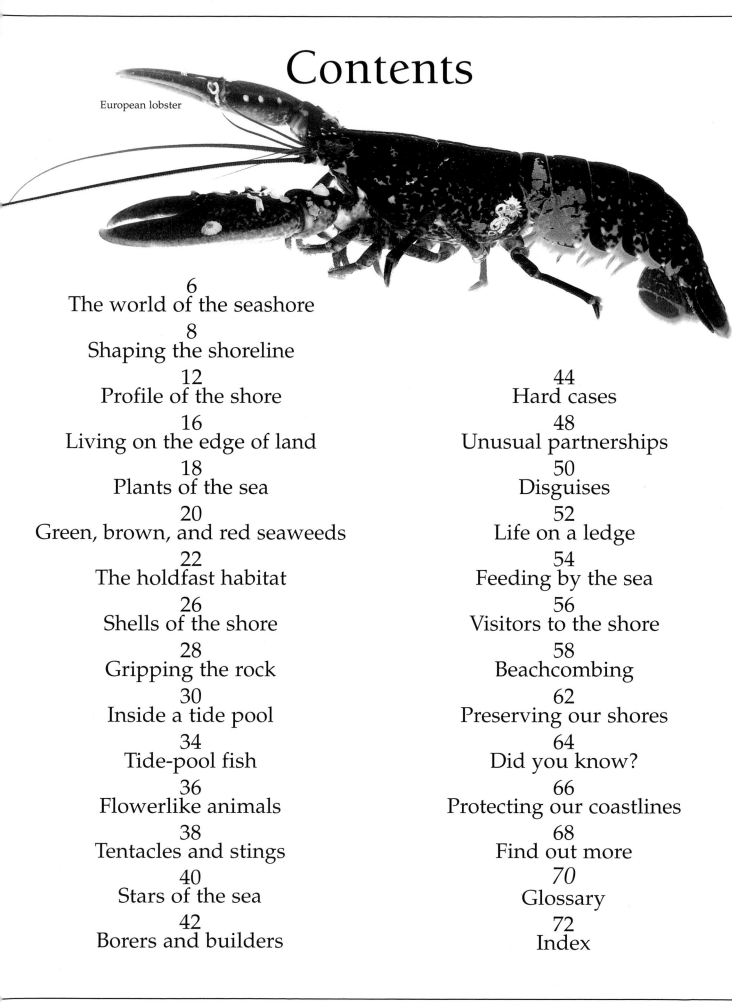

European lobster

The world of the seashore

TWO THIRDS OF OUR PLANET is covered with water.
Every fragment of land, from the great continent
of Eurasia to the tiniest Pacific island, has a shore.
The total length of shorelines is huge. Yet the
width is hardly measurable in comparison - it
is often just a few yards. Shores are strange
places, being the edge of the land as well as the edge
of the sea. The sea level rises and falls with the tides,
making the shore sometimes wet and sometimes
dry. Winds drive unchecked across the open
ocean and hit the coast with great force.
As they blow, they whip up waves that
endlessly crash into the land. No two
stretches of shore are the same. Each is
shaped by many variable factors - the
tides, winds, waves, water currents,
temperature, and climate, and the
types of rock from which the land is
made. Along each shore a group of highly
adapted plants and animals - many
of them strange to our land-
orientated eyes - make their homes.
This book explores the world of
the seashore and describes how
its inhabitants adapt to their
constantly changing
surroundings.

Shaping the shoreline

FOR MILLIONS OF YEARS, every few seconds of each day, waves have hit the seashore. Generated and driven by wind, in calm weather they may be slight ripples, but in a fresh breeze they tumble in foaming heaps onto rocks or sandy beach. In a storm, huge breakers pound the shore like massive hammer blows. Waves erode the shore in three different ways. One is by the hydraulic (water) pressure they exert as they move up the shore and then crash down upon it as they break. A second is by the pneumatic (air) pressure created as water is hurled against rock. It traps pockets of air that are forced into every tiny crack and fissure, like a compressed-air gun. In this way small crevices are widened. Tunnels may be forced along joints in the rock of a low cliff and out at the top, forming blowholes through which each wave shoots spray-filled air. The third way in which waves wear away the land is by corrasion. This is the grinding action of the rocks of all sizes - from giant boulders to tiny sand grains - that are picked up by the waves and flung against the shore. Under this constant barrage, no coastline can remain unchanged.

ON THE WAY TO SAND
The sea gradually wears down large blocks of stone into boulders, then into pebbles, like these, then into sand grains, and finally to tiny particles of silt.

WHO'S WINNING?
The sea is gradually wearing away the land on some stretches of coast. But the land may be slowly rising, too - making the struggle more even. Plants such as marram grass help to reduce erosion on sand dunes by binding the grains with their roots and creating sheltered pockets where other plants can grow.

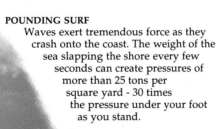

POUNDING SURF
Waves exert tremendous force as they crash onto the coast. The weight of the sea slapping the shore every few seconds can create pressures of more than 25 tons per square yard - 30 times the pressure under your foot as you stand.

RISING TIDE
Time and tide wait for no one, especially picnickers at the seashore who have failed to keep an eye on the water level.

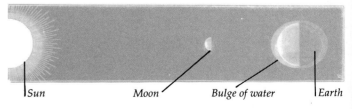

Sun   Moon   Bulge of water   Earth

FORCES FROM SPACE
Twice each day the sea rises up the shore and then goes back out. These movements of water are called tides and are caused by the moon and to a lesser extent, the sun, pulling the earth's water toward them, creating a bulge. When the sun and moon are in line, as shown above, the bulge is the biggest and the tides are at their highest and lowest (p. 12).

As hard as rock?

The type of rock of which the shore is made is one of the chief factors determining the nature of a coastline. Hard rocks such as granites, basalts, and some sandstones are resistant to erosion and often form high headlands (bluffs) and tall, stable cliffs on which plants can root (p. 16).

Granite colored pink by the mineral orthoclase

COARSE OF GRAIN
Granite is an igneous rock; that is, it is formed as molten (liquid) rock cools and the different minerals in it crystallize. Its crystals are relatively large; granite is said to be coarse-grained.

Granite tinted white by the mineral plagioclase

VARIABLE IN COLOR
As granite is worn by the sea and the weather, its less-resistant mineral parts, such as feldspar, change to softer claylike substances. The quartz and mica mineral particles are much harder: they become separated from the soft clay and may eventually become sand on a beach.

VOLCANIC ISLANDS
This lava, from the island of Madeira off northwest Africa, is full of holes created by bubbles of gas trapped as the rock hardened.

Hexagonal columns created by cooling pattern in basalt

Mainland sandstone cliff

LAVA COAST
Some parts of the coast are formed of dark lava flows such as these on the island of Hawaii.

NATURAL COLUMNS
Basalt is another hard igneous rock. It is sometimes worn into startling geometric columns, such as this 230 ft (70 m) deep cave on the west coast of Scotland, known as Fingal's Cave, and the huge "stepping stones" of the Giant's Causeway in Ireland.

Isolated stack of sandstone formed by the collapse of a bridge joining it to the mainland (p. 10)

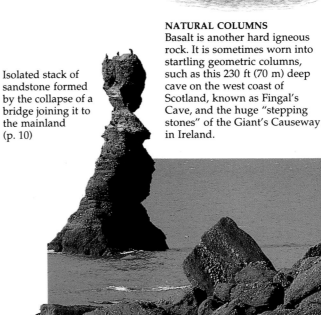

ONCE A BEACH
The grains show clearly in this sample of sandstone. Perhaps on an ancient beach they settled, were cemented together, were then lifted by huge movements of the Earth's crust, and now lie exposed again on a coastal cliff.

Rocks from ancient seas

Many softer rocks, such as chalk and limestone, are sedimentary in origin. They were formed when small particles of calcite (calcium carbonate), which were largely the remains of plants and animals, settled out as sediment on the bottom of an ancient sea. More particles settled on top, and those underneath were gradually squeezed and cemented into solid rock. Sometimes whole plants and animals were trapped in the sediments, and these were gradually turned into rock to become fossils.

WORK OF THE WAVES
As waves approach a headland, they are bent so that they crash into its sides. Headlands made of rocks such as sandstones and limestones may have their lower sides eroded completely, causing an arch to form. In time this becomes a "tower" of rock called a stack.

DISAPPEARING CLIFF
Shores made of soft material such as sand, clay, and other loose particles may be quickly worn down by waves, and the material carried away by currents. On some stretches of shore, wooden barriers called groynes are built to reduce the amount of sediment removed by currents.

THE END OF THE ROAD
Where the coastal rock is soft and crumbly, whole seaside communities have been swallowed by the sea. This road led originally to some houses, whose ruins are now under the waves.

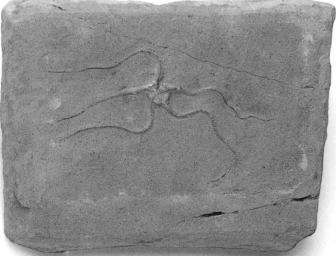

SLOW TO CHANGE
This fossilized brittle star (p. 40) was found at the foot of a cliff. It lived some 200 million years ago, but is very similar to those living today.

GROOVED "PEBBLES"
Hard shells make good fossils. These "pebbles" are brachiopods, or lampshells, which are similar to shellfish like cockles (p. 26). They are common in many sedimentary rocks and help to date the rocks.

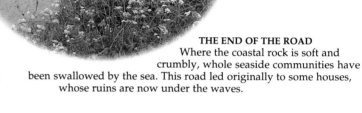

STONE BULLETS
These are the fossilized internal shells of belemnites, prehistoric squidlike mollusks.

Stalks of sea lilies

LACY STALKS
This is a bed of fossilized crinoids or sea lilies, which lived 200 million years ago. Crinoids are animals related to sea stars (p. 40).

WHITE CLIFFS
Chalk is a type of limestone, often dazzling white in color, which may form tall cliffs. Here the various strata (layers) laid down at different times can be seen. At the foot of the cliff, lumps eroded from above are found with pebbles brought by currents from other parts of the coast.

Strata (layers) of chalk laid down at the bottom of an ancient sea

ANCIENT SEA LIFE
Chalk is made of fragments of fossilized microscopic sea plants and animals. Large fossils such as mollusk shells are sometimes embedded in it.

SOLID MUD
Shale is a soft rock which splits easily along its layers and is quickly eroded where it is exposed at the coast. Types that contain the decomposed remains of sea plants and animals are known as oil shale. When heated, oil shale releases a type of crude oil. It may become an important natural resource in the future.

Fossilized shells in limestone

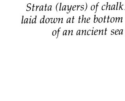

ONCE A SEABED
Limestone sometimes forms breathtaking cliffs, arches, and stacks. This is the 650 ft (200 m) high plateau of the Nullarbor Plain, in southern Australia, which itself was once a seabed. Limestone is a sedimentary rock, often rich in fossils. Lumps may fall from the cliff and split open to reveal remains of prehistoric animals and plants.

Limestone pebbles worn smooth by rubbing against other pebbles on the shore

Profile of the shore

No TWO COASTS are quite the same. But a naturalist can look at an unfamiliar shore (especially a rocky one) and tell at a glance how high the tide rises, how low it falls, whether the area is exposed to wind and waves, or whether it is sheltered. The journey from the edge of the land to the beginning of the sea passes through a series of bands or zones, each with characteristic animals and plants that need to be covered by the sea for different lengths of time. The highest band is the splash or spray zone, which is above the high-water level of the highest tides and is occasionally drenched by spray. Land plants and animals that are adapted to salty conditions live here.

Lichens, which are fungi and algae growing in partnership, are found here as well as a few straying sea snails (p. 26). The lower limit of the splash zone is generally marked by barnacles (p. 44), the first truly marine creatures. The next band is the intertidal ("between the tides") zone, which is regularly covered and uncovered by water. It extends from the barnacles down through the wrack seaweeds (pp. 20-21) to the low-tide area, where larger kelp seaweeds (pp. 22-25) begin to take over.

The third broad band is the subtidal ("below the tides") zone, stretching from the kelp fringe into the permanent shallows.

SAND BINDER
Sandwort's creeping stems and tough roots help it to stabilize loose soil on sand and pebbled shore

SALT'S INCREASING INFLUENCE
The influence of salt water increases from the cliff top, occasionally splashed by storm spray, down through layers that are regularly splashed or sometimes covered by water , to the permanently submerged subtidal zone. Different plants and animals are found in each zone.

High-water mark
of spring tides

THE HIGHEST HIGH TIDE
Every two weeks, the moon and sun are in line with the earth. At this time their gravity pulls with the greatest strength on the sea, and so causes the greatest "bulge" of water (p. 8). This produces the highest high tides and the lowest low tides. They are called spring tides.

High-water mark
of average tides

AVERAGE HIGH TIDE
The upper shore lies around and just below the average high-tide mark, at the upper fringe of the intertidal zone. The high-tide mark itself moves up the beach during the course of a week, finally reaching the spring-tide level. Then it moves gradually back down over the next week. On the upper shore, animals and plants are usually covered by water for one to two hours in each tidal cycle; at a spring high tide they may be covered longer.

BARNACLED BOTTOMS
Feathery-limbed barnacles (right) will settle on any stable surface, including the hulls of ships. Their crusty growths are a problem, as they slow a ship's speed. Special paints have been developed for hulls containing chemicals that stop young barnacles from settling.

A barnacle extends its feathery limbs to grasp and draw food into its mouth, inside the shell plates

FIGHTING IN SLOW MOTION
Limpets are found throughout the intertidal zone. Some species guard their territories to protect their food - a green "garden" of algae (p. 18). Here a light-colored limpet strays onto a neighbor's territory; the occupant crawls over and wedges its shell under the intruder, who then slides away defeated.

Barnacles

The middle and lower shore is shown on pages 14-15

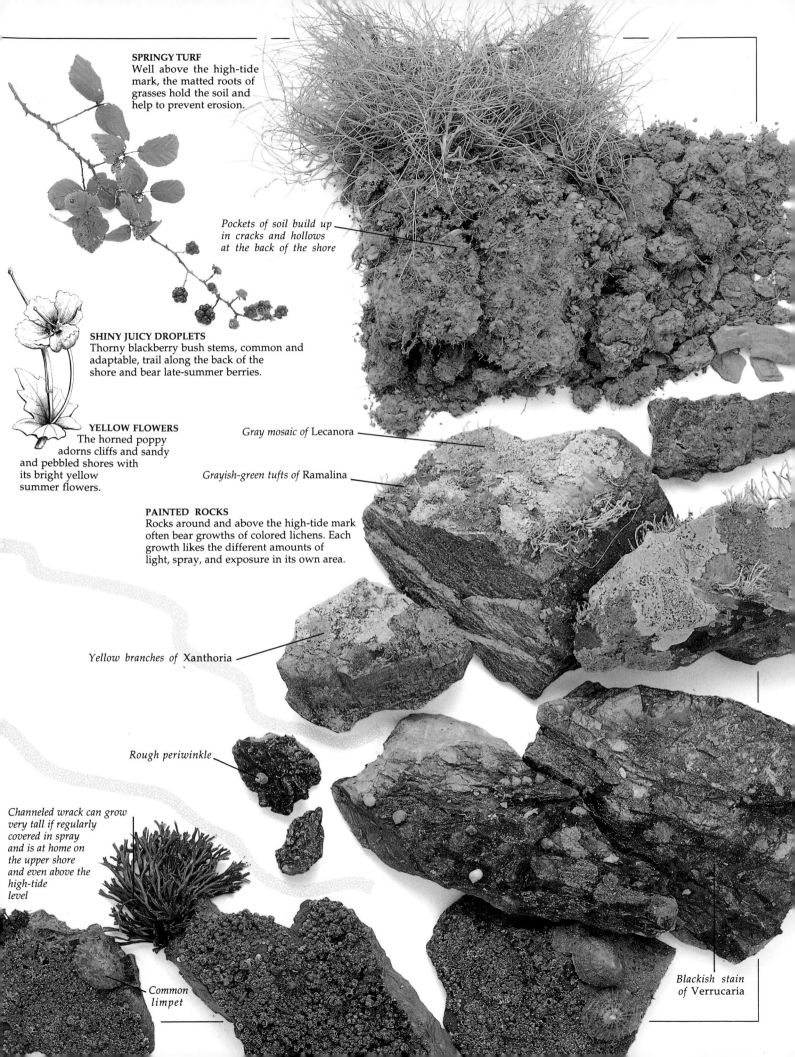

SPRINGY TURF
Well above the high-tide mark, the matted roots of grasses hold the soil and help to prevent erosion.

Pockets of soil build up in cracks and hollows at the back of the shore

SHINY JUICY DROPLETS
Thorny blackberry bush stems, common and adaptable, trail along the back of the shore and bear late-summer berries.

YELLOW FLOWERS
The horned poppy adorns cliffs and sandy and pebbled shores with its bright yellow summer flowers.

Gray mosaic of Lecanora

Grayish-green tufts of Ramalina

PAINTED ROCKS
Rocks around and above the high-tide mark often bear growths of colored lichens. Each growth likes the different amounts of light, spray, and exposure in its own area.

Yellow branches of Xanthoria

Rough periwinkle

Channeled wrack can grow very tall if regularly covered in spray and is at home on the upper shore and even above the high-tide level

Common limpet

Blackish stain of Verrucaria

THE LOWEST HIGH TIDE
Alternating with the spring tides every two weeks are the neap tides. When the moon and sun are at right angles, their gravitational pulls cancel each other out, so there is no very high or very low tide. Any stationary (nonmoving) plant or animal that must be underwater for at least a few minutes on each tide cannot live above the neap high-tide level.

High-water
mark of neap tides

The limpet Patella aspera *is found on the middle and lower shore*

HARSH LICKERS
Purple top shells crawl among the wrack sea-weeds on the middle shore, scraping off tiny algal growths with their filelike tongues.

ROVER ON THE SHORE
The predatory dog whelk roves over most of the shore, feeding on mussels and barnacles.

KELP FANCIERS
These painted top shells graze on the kelp seaweeds of the lower shore.

NO WET FEET
Mussels live in estuaries (places where a river meets the sea) and on more exposed rocky shores, generally on the lower shore below the barnacle belt. Collecting them during spring low tides prevents getting the feet wet.

FIXED ATTACHMENT
The saddle oyster attaches itself to lower-shore and offshore rocks.

OYSTER BORE
The whelk tingle feeds by boring through oyster, mussel, and barnacle shells to reach the flesh.

THE HIGHEST LOW TIDE
Just as neap high tides do not reach very far up the shore, so neap low tides do not run very far down. The tidal range at neaps may be less than half of the range at springs.

Low-water
mark of neap tides

AVERAGE LOW TIDE
The lower shore lies around and just above the average low-tide mark, at the lower fringe of the intertidal zone. Here, life can be sure of always being covered during the neap-tide period.

Low-water
mark of average tides

Large brown kelps are only uncovered at the low water of spring tides

THE BARNACLE BELT
Away from shelter, as exposure to wind and waves increases, the wrack seaweeds have trouble surviving. Their place on the upper and middle rocky shore is taken by the barnacles, which form a distinct belt along many coasts. On some Australian shores, there are more than 120,000 barnacles to the square yard.

Barnacles

SEABORNE FOOD
Many fixed creatures, such as these horse mussels, rely on the sea to bring them food in the form of tiny floating particles.

Mussels encrusted with barnacles and bryozoans

TIDE RIGHT OUT
The best time to study the rocky shore is at low spring tide (p. 63).

Living on the edge of land

APPROACHING THE COAST from inland, we notice how conditions change. There is usually more wind - the sea breeze blows unrestricted across the open ocean. There is also a salty tang to the air, as tiny droplets of seawater are blown off the waves by the wind. Plants growing near the shore must be able to withstand strong winds and, if they are in the splash zone, salt spray. They tend to grow low to the ground to avoid the wind. Another problem plants face, especially on pebbled shores and stony cliff tops, is a shortage of water. Rain soon dries in the breeze or trickles away between the rocks. Some species, such as rock samphire, have thick, fleshy, tough-skinned leaves that store plenty of reserve water. A number of plants that are found on the coast are well adapted to dry habitats and may also grow under similar conditions inland.

THE EDGE OF LAND
Many of the world's people live on or near coasts. The higher and rockier a shoreline, the harder it is for people to visit it, so a greater variety of wildlife is found there.

ROCK-DWELLING LAVENDER
Rock sea lavender is a close relative of the sea lavender of salt marshes, but it is unrelated to the herb lavender.

EVERLASTING THRIFT
Sea pink is another name for wild thrift, which grows in a cushion as protection against the wind. It retains its color when dried and is a favorite with flower arrangers.

Fleshy leaves

Fruit

AT HOME ON STONE
Stonecrops really do grow in dense mats (crops) among stones. After they have flowered, reddish-brown fruits are left on the flowering stems.

SEASIDE MAYWEED
The sea mayweed has daisy-like flowers and fleshy leaves. It flowers in late summer (not May), and grows under cliffs, in barren, rocky ground, and on pebbled shores.

FROM FLOWER TO FRUIT
The tiny, fluffy-looking, yellow-green midsummer flowers of rock samphire have faded and are now developing into brown, "corky" fruits. The juicy leaves of this coastal plant were eaten in the past, either pickled or lightly cooked and served with butter.

Fruit

Each flower has five tiny petals

Fleshy leaves covered by tough skin

Tiny oil glands on undersurfaces of leaves

RED OR WHITE
Red valerian sometimes has white or pink flowers. It is found in rocky places: by the coast on cliffs and pebbled shores and inland on stone walls.

CUSHION OF THYME
Wild thyme is not confined to the coast - it also grows in other dry habitats, such as sand dunes, barren plains, and cliff tops. It has low, creeping stems and it flowers throughout the summer. Like its cultivated relative, wild thyme has a sweet, pungent scent which comes from thymol, its natural aromatic oil.

A collection of scurvy grasses

ANTLER LEAVES
Plantains are tough, stringy, and grow low to the ground, as gardeners well know. The buck's horn plantain is named after its branched antler-like leaves and is common in many coastal areas.

FULL OF VITAMINS
Scurvy grass leaves are rich in vitamin C and were eaten by sailors to ward off the disease scurvy. It is not a grass but a member of the cabbage family.

WITHERED BY WIND
Most trees struggle to grow in the windy and salty conditions on cliff tops over the ocean. This oak has been bent and withered by the wind.

17

Plants of the sea

ALONG THE SHORE - and in the sea itself - are plants quite unlike the familiar trees and flowers that grow on land. Seaweed is their common name, and indeed these plants grow like weeds along many coasts. They are also known as algae. Unlike garden weeds, the algae do not flower and then scatter seeds. They reproduce in a variety of ways, some by means of swollen stem tips which release male and female cells into the water. The algae do not have true roots, stems, or leaves like land plants. But the larger types do have stipes (stems) and fronds (leaves), and sometimes rootlike anchoring holdfasts (pp. 22-23). Most algae also lack a network of tubelike "plumbing" to transport water and dissolved nutrients throughout the plant. Instead they absorb nutrients directly from seawater. The three groups found on rocky shores are green, brown, and red seaweeds.

FEATHERY FRONDS
The delicate structure of many red seaweeds, such as this cockscomb, is best seen when under water. Red seaweeds add splashes of color to the lower shore and the shallows.

SEAWEEDS AT HOME
Seaweeds are difficult to keep in aquariums. Marine salts can help to make "imitation" seawater, but most seaweeds also need constant water movement bringing fresh nutrients and oxygen, and regular tidal cycles that submerge and expose them.

GREEN RIBBONS
Several similar species of *Enteromorpha* thrive on rocky shores. They also grow in estuaries or where a freshwater stream runs over the rocks making the water less salty.

Enteromorpha

INVADER ON THE SHORE
Japanese sargassum has found its way to the United States and elsewhere. It was probably introduced with oyster spat (eggs) imported from Japan. Closely related to this plant are the dense masses of floating seaweed that form in the Sargasso Sea and are occasionally washed on to our shores.

Japanese sargassum

RICH PICKINGS
Shore birds will eat seaweeds, such as *Enteromorpha* and *Ulva*, and will also snap up the small animals sheltering under them. Several species of birds make a living by searching through seaweed beds during low tide.

RED-FEATHERED ROCK DWELLER
Featherweed is a crimson-red seaweed found anchored to rocks in shaded places on the middle and lower shore. Its body branches out into feathery clusters.

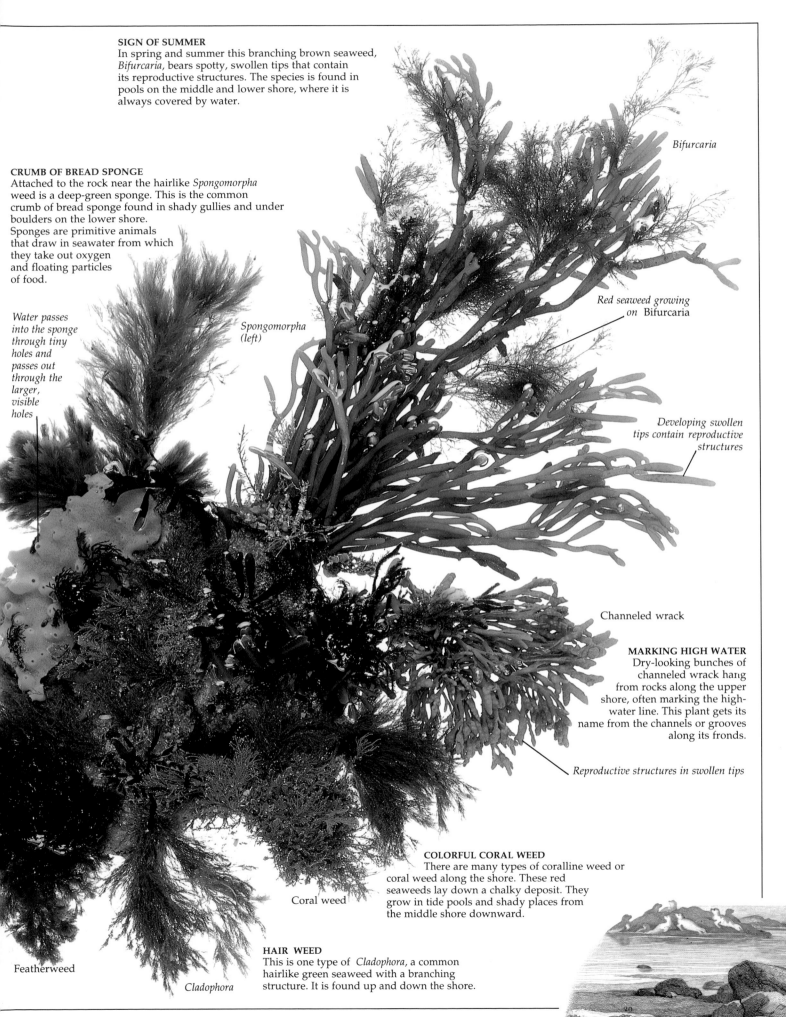

SIGN OF SUMMER
In spring and summer this branching brown seaweed, *Bifurcaria*, bears spotty, swollen tips that contain its reproductive structures. The species is found in pools on the middle and lower shore, where it is always covered by water.

Bifurcaria

CRUMB OF BREAD SPONGE
Attached to the rock near the hairlike *Spongomorpha* weed is a deep-green sponge. This is the common crumb of bread sponge found in shady gullies and under boulders on the lower shore. Sponges are primitive animals that draw in seawater from which they take out oxygen and floating particles of food.

Red seaweed growing on Bifurcaria

Water passes into the sponge through tiny holes and passes out through the larger, visible holes

Spongomorpha (left)

Developing swollen tips contain reproductive structures

Channeled wrack

MARKING HIGH WATER
Dry-looking bunches of channeled wrack hang from rocks along the upper shore, often marking the high-water line. This plant gets its name from the channels or grooves along its fronds.

Reproductive structures in swollen tips

COLORFUL CORAL WEED
There are many types of coralline weed or coral weed along the shore. These red seaweeds lay down a chalky deposit. They grow in tide pools and shady places from the middle shore downward.

Coral weed

Featherweed

HAIR WEED
This is one type of *Cladophora*, a common hairlike green seaweed with a branching structure. It is found up and down the shore.

Cladophora

Green, brown, and red seaweeds

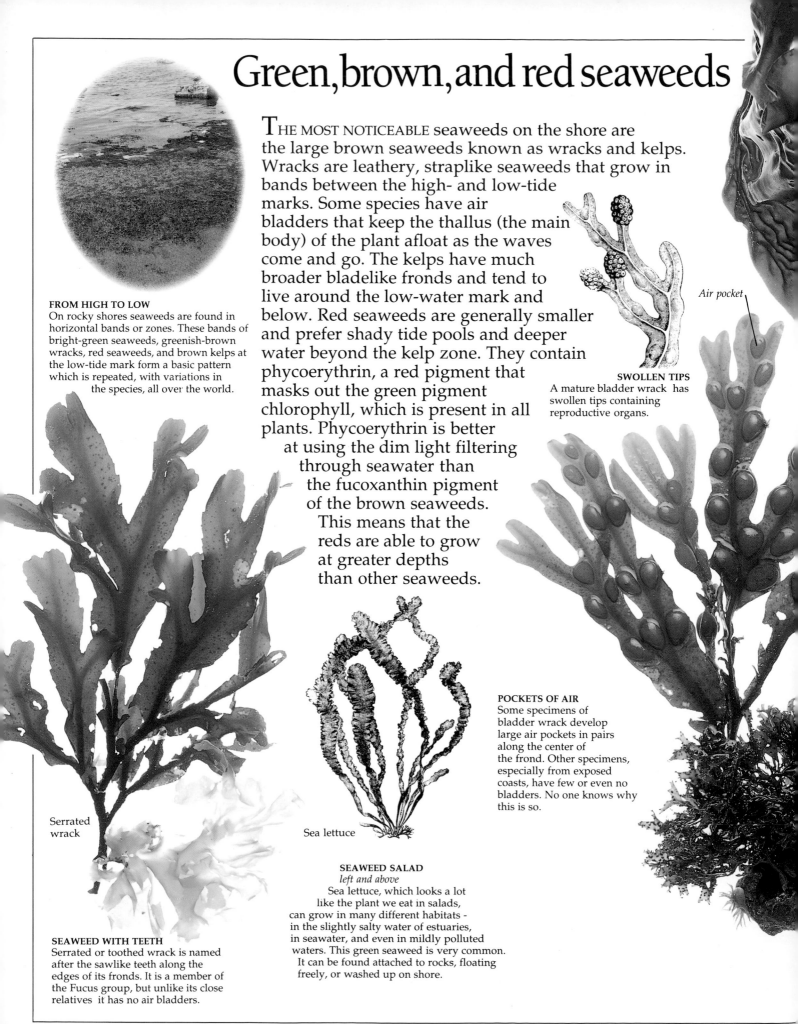

THE MOST NOTICEABLE seaweeds on the shore are the large brown seaweeds known as wracks and kelps. Wracks are leathery, straplike seaweeds that grow in bands between the high- and low-tide marks. Some species have air bladders that keep the thallus (the main body) of the plant afloat as the waves come and go. The kelps have much broader bladelike fronds and tend to live around the low-water mark and below. Red seaweeds are generally smaller and prefer shady tide pools and deeper water beyond the kelp zone. They contain phycoerythrin, a red pigment that masks out the green pigment chlorophyll, which is present in all plants. Phycoerythrin is better at using the dim light filtering through seawater than the fucoxanthin pigment of the brown seaweeds. This means that the reds are able to grow at greater depths than other seaweeds.

FROM HIGH TO LOW
On rocky shores seaweeds are found in horizontal bands or zones. These bands of bright-green seaweeds, greenish-brown wracks, red seaweeds, and brown kelps at the low-tide mark form a basic pattern which is repeated, with variations in the species, all over the world.

Air pocket

SWOLLEN TIPS
A mature bladder wrack has swollen tips containing reproductive organs.

POCKETS OF AIR
Some specimens of bladder wrack develop large air pockets in pairs along the center of the frond. Other specimens, especially from exposed coasts, have few or even no bladders. No one knows why this is so.

Serrated wrack

Sea lettuce

SEAWEED SALAD
left and above
Sea lettuce, which looks a lot like the plant we eat in salads, can grow in many different habitats - in the slightly salty water of estuaries, in seawater, and even in mildly polluted waters. This green seaweed is very common. It can be found attached to rocks, floating freely, or washed up on shore.

SEAWEED WITH TEETH
Serrated or toothed wrack is named after the sawlike teeth along the edges of its fronds. It is a member of the Fucus group, but unlike its close relatives it has no air bladders.

SUGAR AMONG THE SALT
The sugar kelp is a big brown seaweed of the low-water level and below. Its crinkly frond and wavy edges are distinctive, as is the sweet taste of the white powder that forms on its drying surface. It is eaten as a delicacy in the Far East.

LONG THONGS
Sea thong is a leathery, straplike, brown seaweed found near the low-water level. Its narrow fronds may grow more than 10 ft (3 m) long. Like many seaweeds, it has a tough, rubbery texture to protect it as the waves pound it against the rocks.

Sugar kelp

Sea thong

BUTTON-SHAPED BASE
The button- or mushroom-shaped base is one stage in the life cycle of the sea thong. In the plant's second year of growth, the thongs develop from this base and contain the reproductive structures.

Bladder wrack

TWO RED WEEDS
Carrageen (left) and dulse (below) are both red seaweeds that are harvested commercially. Carrageen provides a gel for jellies; dulse can be eaten raw, cooked as a vegetable, or added to stews and soups.

Carrageen

Dulse

The holdfast habitat

SEAWEEDS do not have true roots. The gnarled, rootlike structures of large brown seaweeds are called, appropriately, holdfasts. They hold tight to the rock and provide anchorage, like a tree's roots in the soil. Unlike true roots, the rootlets of a holdfast do not take up water or nutrients; instead these are absorbed through the whole surface of the seaweed. However, holdfasts do provide shelter on the shore. Just as trees protect a woodland's interior from wind, driving rain, and hot sun, leathery fronds and tough holdfasts shield the low-shore kelp forests from the sun and the force of the waves and wind. Many smaller plants and numerous shore animals, such as crabs, fish, prawns, and mollusks, take advantage of the calmer conditions within the forests of brown seaweeds. During storms, weaker seaweeds are torn from the rocks. In the storm's aftermath, huge mounds of kelp are found on the shore, often with their inhabitants still clinging to the fronds. The California sea otter (p. 56) is a well-known inhabitant of the kelp beds of the Pacific coast. When it rests on the surface, it secures itself by wrapping kelp fronds around its body.

Mussels indicate that the seaweed is at least several years old

HOLDING FAST
Oarweeds, sometimes called cuvie or forest kelp, firmly grip the rock with the finger-like rootlets of their holdfasts. Other brown seaweeds, as well as red and green species, have colonized this small piece of slate. Their bases have grown into every crack and cranny in the rock.

Young oarweeds

FLATTENED KELP DWELLER
The porcelain crab is a filter feeder and more closely related to hermit crabs (pp. 48-49) and lobsters than true crabs. Its walking legs have sharp spines that help it to grip smooth rock or slippery holdfasts with ease, enabling it to slide its flat body under boulders or into hollows among the holdfast rootlets.

Porcelain crab

CUTAWAY HIDEAWAY
A section cut through the side of a holdfast (right) shows its tough and stringy structure. It also reveals a tiny "cave" where the porcelain crab (above) shelters.

FRILLS AND FURBELOWS
One of the most distinctive brown seaweeds is furbelows. Its stipe (stem) has wavy edges and divides into long fanlike fronds that may grow to 6 ft (2 m) or more.

Furbelows

Hollow underside

Rootlets of holdfast

PLANT OR PLASTIC?
Like other large kelps, furbelows grows at the low-tide level and below. Its holdfast is covered in growths that look like bubble-filled plastic packaging. The holdfast grows in one year, which means this plant is an annual.

DRYING THE SHORE'S HARVEST
Seaweeds are nutritious plants, especially rich in some vitamins and minerals such as iodine. In many regions they are eaten regularly as a side dish or chopped and grated as garnish. In Japan kelp and laver (a red seaweed) are cultivated and sold as kombu and nori respectively.

TUG-OF-WAR WITH THE WAVES
Similar species of coastal kelps are found around the world. This holdfast anchors a *Macrocystis* (a type of giant kelp) from New Zealand. The entire plant is tens of yards long. Waves and water currents pull on the enormous fronds with great force, so the holdfast must be equal to the challenge. More than 600 species of seaweeds have been recorded in New Zealand waters.

The rest of the kelp is shown on the next page

A SHARP TONGUE
Blue-rayed limpets commonly graze on kelps, scraping away at the seaweed and any plants and animals crusted on it. Sometimes this mollusk erodes a "home base" (p. 29) in the holdfast.

Red seaweeds growing on kelp

Porcelain crab in hollow of holdfast

CLEANING THE KELP
The common sea urchin is one of many shore creatures that graze the rocks and seaweeds. Using its powerful jaws (p. 28), the urchin scrapes the rocks and kelp stipes clean, eating small algal growths and tiny settled animals. Sometimes too many urchins occur and strip away all new growth from the rocks, leaving them bare and lifeless.

Blade base splits into fronds

Stipe of kelp

GIANT SEAWEEDS
The *Macrocystis*, or giant kelp, makes up the California kelp forests, home of the sea otter (p. 56). Some types of giant kelp may grow 3 ft (1 m) in a day under good conditions and reach lengths of 325 ft (100 m).

Ends of fronds are
decaying

Scar tissue formed over wounds
caused by feeding animals

Coastal rowers may get their oars
tangled in the oarweed
forests

LACY MATS
The lacy
patterns seen on
some kelps are called bryozoans. They are made up of
many tiny compartments with
an individual animal
in each.

Dogfish lay their eggs
among seaweed (p. 61)

25

Shells of the shore

Eight jointed shell plates

ON THE SEASHORE many of the animals that live inside shells are mollusks. They are commonly known as shellfish. Mollusks are an enormous and varied animal group, with over 120,000 species worldwide. The typical mollusk has a soft body, a muscular foot on which it moves, and a hard shell made of calcium carbonate and other minerals taken from seawater; but there are many variations. On the shore the group includes gastropods (snail-like mollusks) such as limpets, abalones, top shells, nerites, periwinkles, conches, whelks, cowries, and cone shells.

Most of the edible mollusks are bivalves, which have two parts, or valves, to the shell. These include cockles, mussels, scallops, clams, oysters, razor clams, and ship worms. Tusk shells, chitons, sea slugs, squid, and octopuses also belong to the mollusk group.

SHE SELLS SEASHELLS
The beauty and hardness of sea-shells has made them favorites for jewelery and for gifts such as the decorative shell boxes sold by the little girl in the picture. In some coastal areas certain shells were used as currency, such as the "money cowries" of tropical islands.

TEETH OF IRON
Chitons (p. 28) are common mollusks on many rocky shores, but are difficult to spot because they blend in with the rocks. This species is a mid-shore seaweed grazer from the Indian Ocean. Its tiny teeth are capped with a hard substance that contains iron and keeps them from wearing down.

STRIPES AND SPOTS
Top shells, with their striped and spotted cone-shaped shells, are bright and familiar inhabitants of tide pools (pp. 30-33). This species lives in the Red Sea and grazes on algae on the lower shore.

PEARLY INSIDE
Abalones are known for the beautiful, rainbow-sheen mother-of-pearl on the inside of their shells. These relatives of top shells and limpets graze on algae and are them-selves eaten as a seafood delicacy, especially in western North America (where this species comes from) and the South Pacific.

Waste water is expelled through these holes

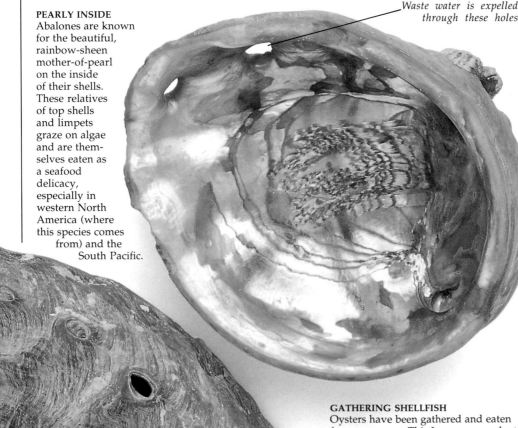

DEEP-DOWN SHINE
The serpent's-head cowrie is common around many shores of the Indian and Pacific Oceans, including all but the south coast of Australia. It crops small algae from the rocks and the outer edges of coral reefs, where the surf breaks. The animal withdraws into the slit on the shell's underside when in danger.

GATHERING SHELLFISH
Oysters have been gathered and eaten for many years. This Japanese woodcut print shows oyster fishermen at work near the sacred twin rocks in Ise Bay.

LIKE A PATTERNED TOY TOP

Monodonta is another boldly patterned top shell from the Indian Ocean. Top shells belong to the gastropod group of mollusks. Gastropod means "stomach-foot" and these animals, like their snail cousins, appear to slide along on their bellies.

RAW IN ITS JUICE

The oyster's two shells are held firmly together by a strong muscle. To get at the flesh, the shells must be pried open with a knife. Oysters are often eaten raw in their natural juices, straight from the shell.

SHORE HERBIVORE

Nerites are found on many tropical coasts - these are from the Caribbean, where they live on the middle shore. These gastropods are herbivores (plant eaters); they scrape tiny algae from rocks, roots, and large seaweeds.

Spine for prying apart the plates of a barnacle

THE PREDATORY WHELK

Unlike many dog whelks, the Chilean dog whelk is not snail-shaped but more limpet-like and has a very large foot. It patrols the middle and lower shore of South America's Pacific coast, preying on barnacles and mussels.

FILTERING THE SEA

There are many species of oysters from different regions. This one, the rock oyster, cements itself to the rock, usually by its right-hand shell. Like many of its bivalve relatives, the oyster is a filter feeder. It draws in a current of seawater, filters out tiny floating food particles, and passes these into its digestive system, using tiny beating hairs called cilia.

SHORE CARNIVORE

Dog whelks, like nerites (above), are gastropods, but unlike the nerites they are carnivores (meat eaters). This species, from North America's west coast, uses its spine to pry apart the plates of a barnacle and reach the flesh within.

MOLLUSK WITH DART

The Hebrew cone from the Indian and Pacific oceans is an intertidal species (p. 12) belonging to the cone shells, a large group of gastropods. Cone shells have tiny poison "darts," harpoon-like structures that are fired into worms and other prey to paralyze them.

WORM-HUNTING WHELK

The red-mouthed drupe is another type of dog whelk, named for its reddish "mouth" or shell opening. This species comes from the Indo-Pacific region, where it feeds on worms on the lower shore.

European cowries, smaller than their tropical counterparts, feed on seasquirts on the lower shore

MUSSEL PROTECTION

Like its common relative the blue mussel, the green mussel attaches itself to rocks and pilings by tough threads called byssus. This species is found in Southeast Asia. Mussels are collected for food and bait.

SEA FOOD

In a clambake, depicted here by the 19th-century American artist Winslow Homer, the clams are cooked in a steaming bed of seaweed over hot stones.

Gripping the rock

ROCKY SEASHORES can be very harsh habitats as waves pound unyielding stone. Many intertidal creatures have responded by evolving hard outer shells, which also protect them from predators and the sun's drying heat. Mollusks such as limpets have low, volcano-shaped shells that present little resistance to waves. The periwinkle's shell is thick, tough, and rounded; if it is detached it soon rolls to rest in a gully. Another aid to survival is a good grip. Sea stars and sea urchins have hundreds of tiny tube feet; limpets and sea snails have a single large suction foot.

GRIPPING BY A STALK
Goose barnacles, which are often washed up on the shore, have tough stalks to grip any floating debris such as wood or pumice stone. These crustaceans (p. 44) live at sea, filtering tiny food particles from the water like their rock-bound shore relatives (p. 12). Once people believed that these barnacles hatched into geese - perhaps because their frilly limbs looked like feathers, or maybe to explain the mysterious disappearance of the geese in winter.

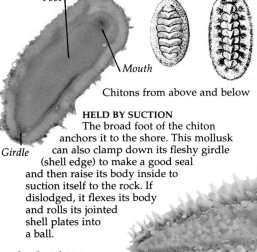

Foot

Mouth

Girdle

Chitons from above and below

HELD BY SUCTION
The broad foot of the chiton anchors it to the shore. This mollusk can also clamp down its fleshy girdle (shell edge) to make a good seal and then raise its body inside to suction itself to the rock. If dislodged, it flexes its body and rolls its jointed shell plates into a ball.

ANCHORED BY FEET
The five-rayed symmetry (evenness) of the common sea urchin shows that it is a cousin of the sea star. It is protected by sharp spines that can be tilted on ball-and-socket joints at their bases. It uses its long tube feet to anchor itself to the rock, drag itself along, seize bits of food, and get rid of debris.

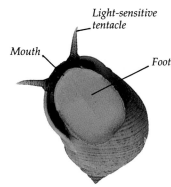

Light-sensitive tentacle

Mouth

Foot

SEALING UP THE CRACKS
Edible or common periwinkles have long been gathered from the lower shore for food. Like its land relation, the snail, the periwinkle moves on a muscular, fleshy foot lubricated by a film of mucus. When not walking, it often nestles in a crack or gully and seals the gap between its shell and the rock with mucus.

Sea urchin's test

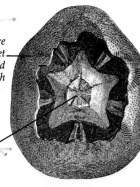

Holes where tube feet passed through

Mouth (Aristotle's lantern)

Anchoring tube feet

Tube feet searching water

Underside of common sea urchin

THE INNER URCHIN
When the spines and skin are removed, the beautifully patterned test (internal shell) of the sea urchin is revealed. The system of five lever-operated teeth with which the urchin grazes on seaweeds is called Aristotle's lantern.

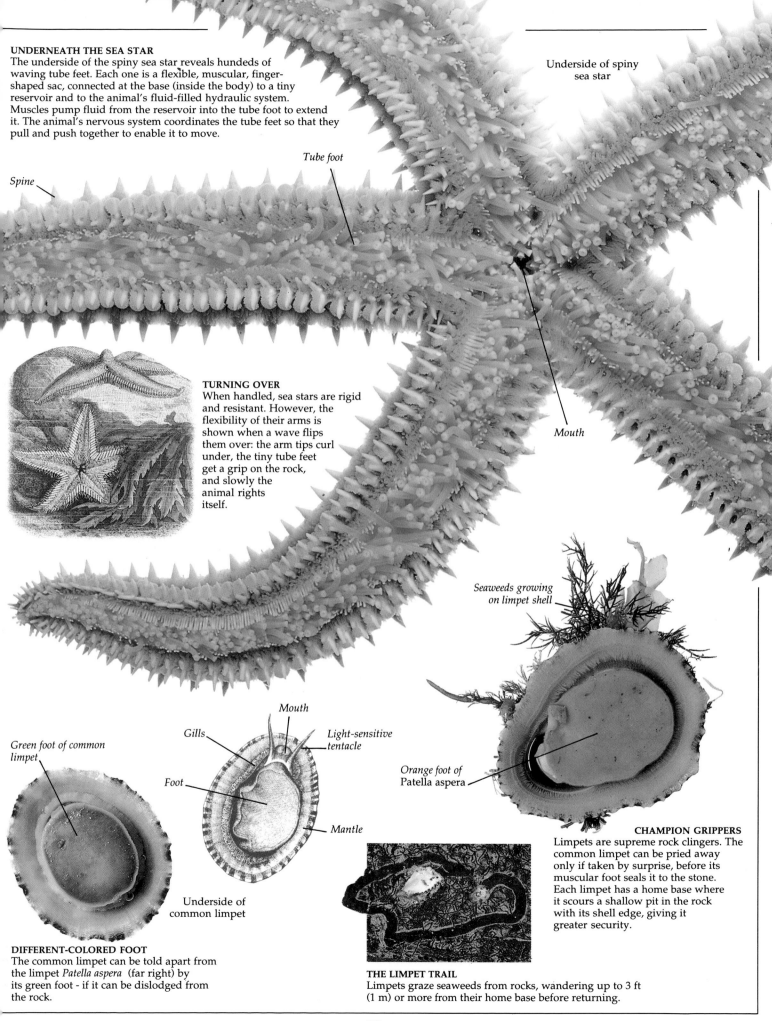

UNDERNEATH THE SEA STAR
The underside of the spiny sea star reveals hundeds of waving tube feet. Each one is a flexible, muscular, finger-shaped sac, connected at the base (inside the body) to a tiny reservoir and to the animal's fluid-filled hydraulic system. Muscles pump fluid from the reservoir into the tube foot to extend it. The animal's nervous system coordinates the tube feet so that they pull and push together to enable it to move.

Tube foot

Spine

Underside of spiny
sea star

TURNING OVER
When handled, sea stars are rigid and resistant. However, the flexibility of their arms is shown when a wave flips them over: the arm tips curl under, the tiny tube feet get a grip on the rock, and slowly the animal rights itself.

Mouth

*Seaweeds growing
on limpet shell*

Mouth

Gills

*Light-sensitive
tentacle*

*Green foot of common
limpet*

Foot

*Orange foot of
Patella aspera*

Mantle

CHAMPION GRIPPERS
Limpets are supreme rock clingers. The common limpet can be pried away only if taken by surprise, before its muscular foot seals it to the stone. Each limpet has a home base where it scours a shallow pit in the rock with its shell edge, giving it greater security.

Underside of
common limpet

DIFFERENT-COLORED FOOT
The common limpet can be told apart from the limpet *Patella aspera* (far right) by its green foot - if it can be dislodged from the rock.

THE LIMPET TRAIL
Limpets graze seaweeds from rocks, wandering up to 3 ft (1 m) or more from their home base before returning.

Inside a tide pool

A TIDE POOL is a natural world in miniature - a specialized habitat in which plants and animals live together. A wide range of plants is found here, from the film of microscopic algae coating almost any bare surface, to wracks and other large seaweeds. These plants capture light energy from the sun and obtain nutrients from seawater. They provide food for periwinkles, limpets, and other plant eaters. Flesh-eating animals such as sea stars, small fish, whelks, and other creatures eat the plant eaters. And then there are crabs, prawns, and other scavengers that eat both plant and animal material. Filter feeders such as barnacles and mussels consume tiny particles of floating food, which may be miniature animals and plants, or bits of long-dead larger organisms.

NATURE STUDY
Naturalists have always been fascinated by tide pools. The great 19th-century English naturalist Philip Gosse studied shore life in Devon, in southwest England. His son Edmund described how his father would "wade breast-high into one of the huge pools and examine the worm-eaten surface of the rock. . .there used often to lurk a marvellous profusion of animal and vegetable forms."

STRINGS OF EGGS
Sea hares come to the shore in spring and summer to browse on the seaweeds and lay their pinkish purple, stringlike spawn.

SLUGS OF THE SEA
Tide pools occasionally trap sluglike creatures, such as this *Hypselodoris* from Guam, in the Pacific. They are called sea slugs or nudibranchs, a name that means "naked gills," after the feathery tufts on their backs which absorb oxygen from seawater. Sea slugs (like land slugs) are mollusks without shells.

TENTACLES LIKE A HARE'S EARS?
The sea hare is not considered a true sea slug, since it has a thin, flexible shell under the folds on its back.

RECYCLED STINGS
Some sea slugs are equipped with stinging cells absorbed from anemones that they eat.

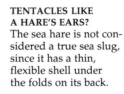

SPONGE EATER
The sea lemon has a mottled yellowish body. It feeds on crumb of bread sponges (p. 19).

NOT RECOMMENDED
The bright colors of many sea slugs warn potential predators that they taste horrible.

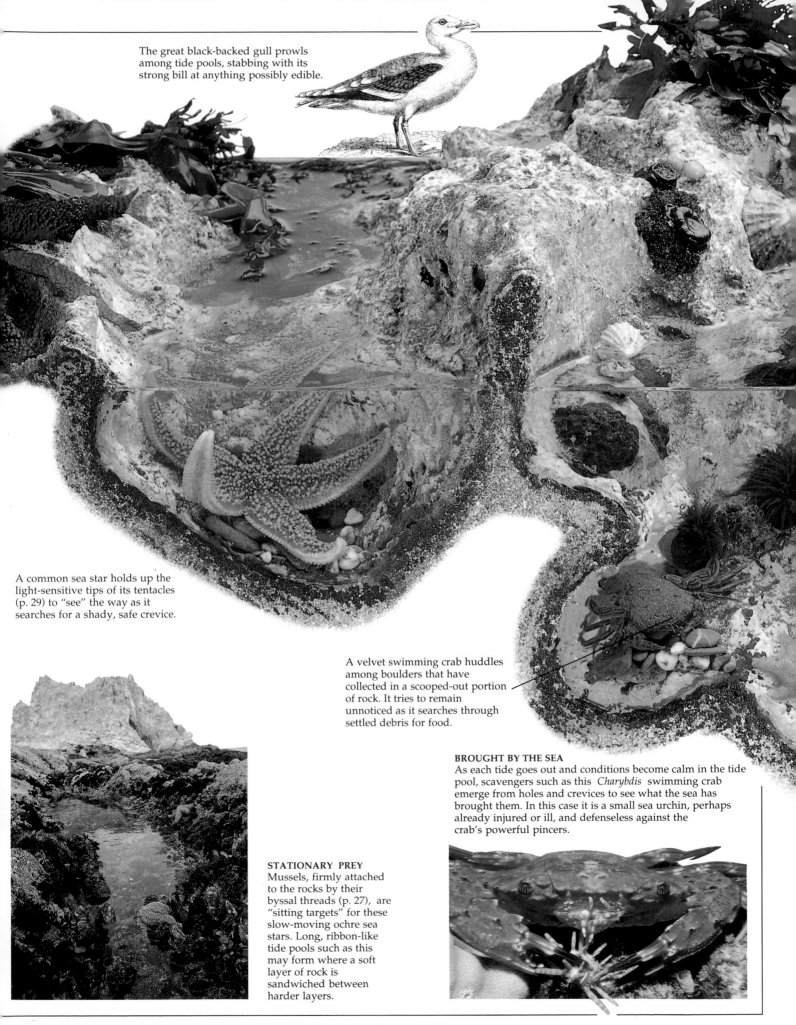

The great black-backed gull prowls among tide pools, stabbing with its strong bill at anything possibly edible.

A common sea star holds up the light-sensitive tips of its tentacles (p. 29) to "see" the way as it searches for a shady, safe crevice.

A velvet swimming crab huddles among boulders that have collected in a scooped-out portion of rock. It tries to remain unnoticed as it searches through settled debris for food.

BROUGHT BY THE SEA
As each tide goes out and conditions become calm in the tide pool, scavengers such as this *Charybdis* swimming crab emerge from holes and crevices to see what the sea has brought them. In this case it is a small sea urchin, perhaps already injured or ill, and defenseless against the crab's powerful pincers.

STATIONARY PREY
Mussels, firmly attached to the rocks by their byssal threads (p. 27), are "sitting targets" for these slow-moving ochre sea stars. Long, ribbon-like tide pools such as this may form where a soft layer of rock is sandwiched between harder layers.

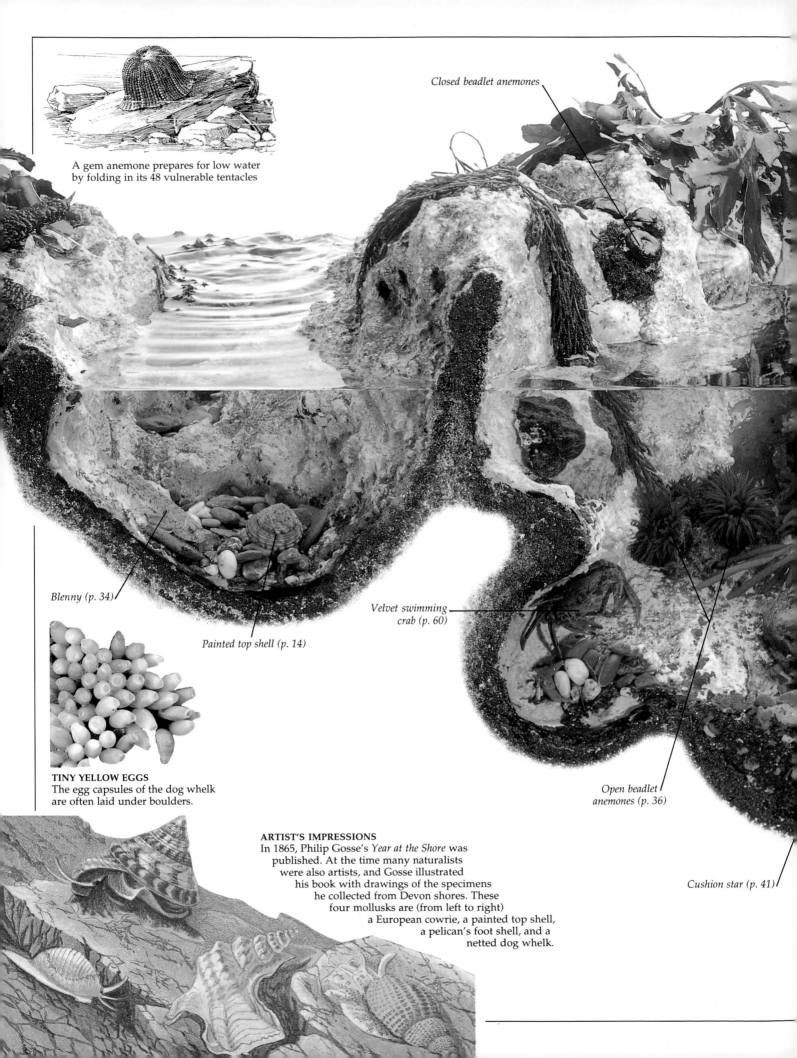

A gem anemone prepares for low water by folding in its 48 vulnerable tentacles

Closed beadlet anemones

Blenny (p. 34)

Painted top shell (p. 14)

TINY YELLOW EGGS
The egg capsules of the dog whelk are often laid under boulders.

Velvet swimming crab (p. 60)

Open beadlet anemones (p. 36)

Cushion star (p. 41)

ARTIST'S IMPRESSIONS
In 1865, Philip Gosse's *Year at the Shore* was published. At the time many naturalists were also artists, and Gosse illustrated his book with drawings of the specimens he collected from Devon shores. These four mollusks are (from left to right) a European cowrie, a painted top shell, a pelican's foot shell, and a netted dog whelk.

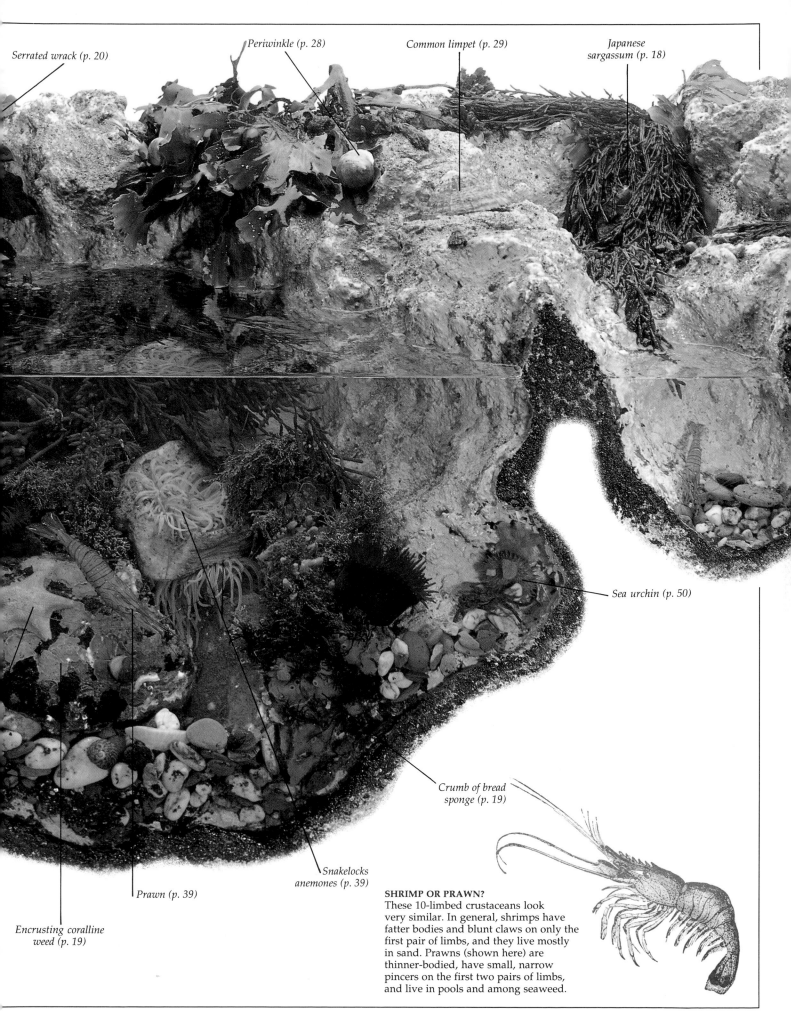

Serrated wrack (p. 20)

Periwinkle (p. 28)

Common limpet (p. 29)

Japanese sargassum (p. 18)

Sea urchin (p. 50)

Crumb of bread sponge (p. 19)

Snakelocks anemones (p. 39)

Prawn (p. 39)

Encrusting coralline weed (p. 19)

SHRIMP OR PRAWN?
These 10-limbed crustaceans look very similar. In general, shrimps have fatter bodies and blunt claws on only the first pair of limbs, and they live mostly in sand. Prawns (shown here) are thinner-bodied, have small, narrow pincers on the first two pairs of limbs, and live in pools and among seaweed.

Tide-pool fish

LIFE FOR SMALL ANIMALS such as the tiny fish that live in tide pools is full of danger. If it rains heavily, the seawater in a small pool is greatly diluted, so that for a few hours the fish (and other inhabitants) must adjust their body chemistry to cope with the lower concentration of salt. The falling tide may maroon them in a shallow puddle, so that they have to wriggle across bare rock to the safety of a deeper pool. In an hour, the sun can turn a cool pool into a warm bath, causing animals to leave the water and find refuge under a cool, moist rock rather than suffer a form of heatstroke. At low tide, gulls feed on tide-pool inhabitants; on the returning tide, small creatures can be crushed by rolling boulders. Fish predators are a constant threat: conger eels lurk in crevices, and hungry bass follow the tide in, snapping up any stragglers. The fish shown here have to be hardy creatures to survive the constantly changing conditions and physical threats in the miniature habitat of the tide pool.

A FLICK OF THE FINS
There are about 1,500 species in the goby family, most of them small, flat, tough-looking shore dwellers. These are sand gobies, which can cover themselves in sand with a flick of their fins.

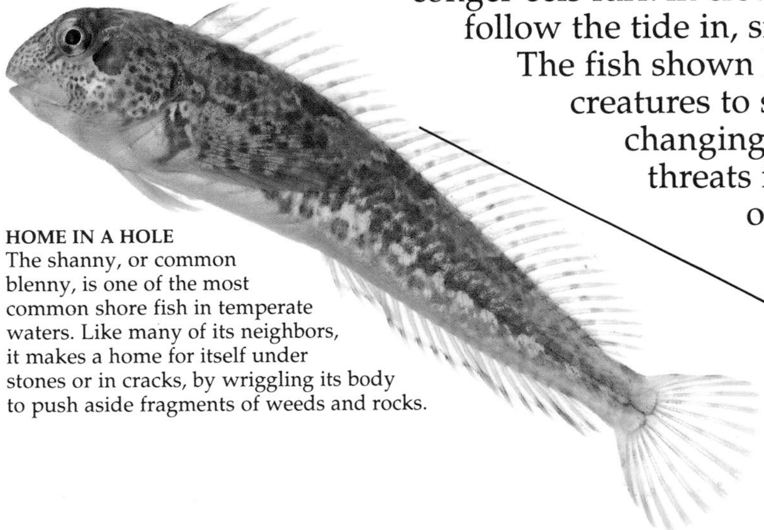

DANGER AFOOT
Many shore creatures are so well camouflaged that they are unseen by walkers on the shore, and must dart away from a descending foot.

HOME IN A HOLE
The shanny, or common blenny, is one of the most common shore fish in temperate waters. Like many of its neighbors, it makes a home for itself under stones or in cracks, by wriggling its body to push aside fragments of weeds and rocks.

Distinctive dip in the middle of the dorsal (back) fin

Dark spots along the base of the dorsal fin

LIKE AN EEL
The butterfish has a distinctive row of spots along its back. It lives on North Atlantic shores, from the U.S. to Britain and mainland Europe. Its common name comes from the feel of its slimy, slippery body.

LOOKING UPWARD
Shore fish have eyes which are closer to the tops of their heads than many other fish. This enables them to watch for predators from above, such as sea birds.

Shanny

Butterfish

Blenny

SPOTTED GOLD
The dark spots on the front of the dorsal fin and upper tail identify the goldsinny, a member of the numerous and varied wrasse group. Large individuals reach about 8 in (20 cm) in length.

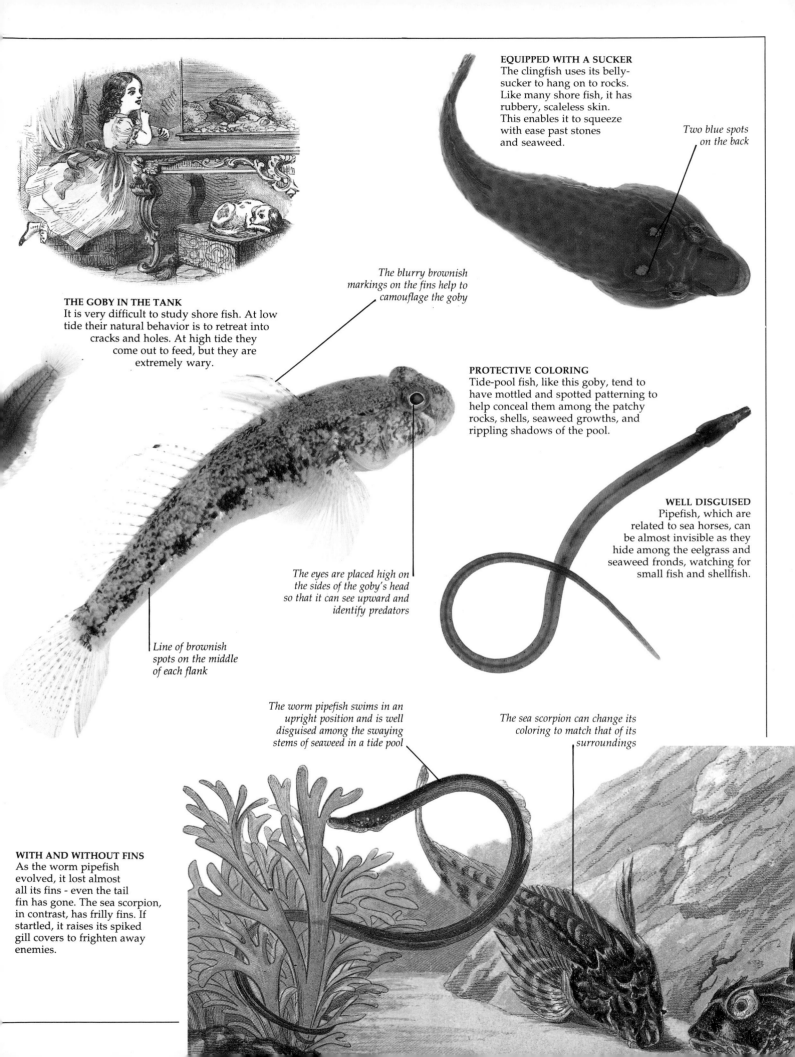

EQUIPPED WITH A SUCKER
The clingfish uses its belly-sucker to hang on to rocks. Like many shore fish, it has rubbery, scaleless skin. This enables it to squeeze with ease past stones and seaweed.

Two blue spots on the back

The blurry brownish markings on the fins help to camouflage the goby

THE GOBY IN THE TANK
It is very difficult to study shore fish. At low tide their natural behavior is to retreat into cracks and holes. At high tide they come out to feed, but they are extremely wary.

PROTECTIVE COLORING
Tide-pool fish, like this goby, tend to have mottled and spotted patterning to help conceal them among the patchy rocks, shells, seaweed growths, and rippling shadows of the pool.

WELL DISGUISED
Pipefish, which are related to sea horses, can be almost invisible as they hide among the eelgrass and seaweed fronds, watching for small fish and shellfish.

The eyes are placed high on the sides of the goby's head so that it can see upward and identify predators

Line of brownish spots on the middle of each flank

The worm pipefish swims in an upright position and is well disguised among the swaying stems of seaweed in a tide pool

The sea scorpion can change its coloring to match that of its surroundings

WITH AND WITHOUT FINS
As the worm pipefish evolved, it lost almost all its fins - even the tail fin has gone. The sea scorpion, in contrast, has frilly fins. If startled, it raises its spiked gill covers to frighten away enemies.

Flower-like animals

ANEMONES are the surprising "flowers" of the shore - surprising because they are not flowers at all. They are hollow, jelly-like animals belonging to a group called the coelenterates or cnidarians, which also includes jellyfish and corals. Their "petals" are actually tentacles with special stinging cells that poison their prey. The prey is then pulled toward the mouth (p. 39). Like flowers, anemones have evolved many colors, from salmon pink to emerald green and jet black. In many there is great color variation even within the same species. Another remarkable feature is that many can move, if only slowly, sliding their muscular bases along the rock surface. Certain species burrow in sand and gravel; others slide their bodies into crevices in the rocks so that only their tentacles show. As the tide ebbs most anemones on the shore pull in their tentacles and become jelly-like blobs to avoid drying out.

OPEN FOR DINNER
Beautiful but deadly: the waving tentacles of an anemone colony are a forest of danger for small sea creatures.

Mouth in center of body

TRAFFIC-LIGHT ANEMONES
Beadlet anemones come in various colors, including red, amber, and green. When the tide recedes, they fold in their tentacles, looking like overgrown gumdrops scattered on the rocks. When fully grown they have about 200 tentacles.

SWEEPING THE SEA
Fan worms are sometimes mistaken for anemones, but they belong to a different group of animals - the annelids (which include earthworms). The tentacles of the "fan" filter tiny food particles from the water but withdraw into the tube in a flash if danger threatens.

BLEMISH OR BEAUTY?
The wartlike knobs on this creature's body have led to one of its common names - wartlet anemone. The warts can be seen on the closed wartlet anemone on the opposite. page

Calcareous (chalky) algae encrusting rock

"FLOWER" ON A "STALK"
This side view of a grayish beadlet anemone shows its stubby "stalk" (body) with a rainbow-like sheen around the base. Beadlets can survive being out of water for some time and can live very high on the shore.

FEATHERY PLUMES
The plumose or frilled anemone is brown, reddish, or white and may grow up to 1 ft (30 cm) tall. Its feathery tentacles catch very small bits of food and waft them down to the mouth by the beating action of tiny hairs called cilia.

Snow-white tentacles and brown body of a beadlet anemone

Living cup coral with tentacles extended

Chalky skeleton of dead cup coral

PINK-TIPPED TENTACLES
Snakelocks anemones range in color from gray with delicate sheens of pink or green to all-over deep green. The pink-tipped tentacles do not withdraw in this species even when it is out of water.

LIVING CORAL
Corals are similar to anemones and are members of the same group, the coelenterates (cnidarians). This cup coral lives alone, unlike its tropical reef-building cousins.

Side view of dead cup coral

The body "warts" of this wartlet anemone are visible in this closed-up individual

Strings (acontia) of stinging cells

TINY GHOSTS
There are many different species of these tiny, ghost-white encrusting anemones covering some areas of rocky shore.

GIANT OF ITS KIND
The giant green anemone of tropical waters is one of the largest anemones in the world. It may grow to more than 3 ft (1 m) across.

MINIATURE FANS
Fan worms (see opposite page) live inside protective, chalky tubes. Some species live buried in the mud; others attach themselves to rocks, like this one. Look to the left - can you spot another small fan worm on the opposite corner of this stone?

STINGING STRINGS
The colorful sagartia anemone is one of several species that feeds and defends itself by shooting pale strings of stinging cells through its mouth or through slits in its body. The "strings" are in fact parts of the animal's guts!

Encrusted remains of barnacle shells

Coiled, chalky remains of tube worm

Tentacles and stings

KRAKEN AHOY
The kraken, a sea monster of Norse legend, made short work of ships and their crews. As is often the case, the fable has some basis in fact. The kraken looks suspiciously like the squid, a member of the mollusk group. Atlantic giant squid have been recorded up to 50 ft (15 m) long, including tentacles, and weighing two tons. Their remains are sometimes found washed up on the shore (p. 56).

THE COELENTERATE (CNIDARIAN) ANIMALS (jellyfish, anemones, and corals) are the stingers of the shore. These creatures do not not have brains or complex sense organs such as eyes and ears. Unable to move quickly, they cannot escape from predators or pursue prey. Instead, they protect themselves and capture food with tiny stinging cells in their tentacles. Inside each cell is a capsule called a nematocyst, which contains a long, coiled thread. In some species these are barbed, in others they contain venom. Triggered by touch or by certain chemicals, the threads flick out and then either the barbs hold on to the prey, or venom is injected into it. Then the animal drags its victim into the digestive cavity within the body. Some jellyfish have extremely powerful venom that can cause great pain to swimmers who brush against them. Their nematocysts remain active for a while even after the animal is washed up and dies on the shore. The best known jellyfish is the Portuguese man-of-war. This is not a true jellyfish, but a colony of small animals from the same group. A swimmer may be stung without ever seeing the creature responsible, since the tentacles trail in the current several yards behind the floating body. The box jellyfish, or sea wasp, of tropical waters has tentacles up to 33 ft (10 m) long and its sting is lethal to humans.

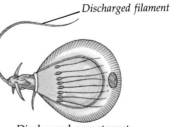

Common prawn

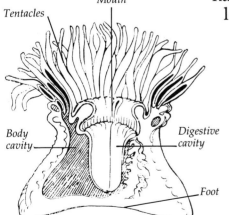

Mouth
Tentacles
Body cavity
Digestive cavity
Foot

INSIDE AN ANEMONE
Anemones, and their coelenterate (cnidarian) relatives, are simply constructed creatures. The ring of tentacles surrounds a mouth that leads to the digestive cavity inside the body. Prey is pushed into the cavity, digested, and absorbed, and any remains excreted through the mouth.

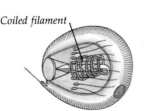

Coiled filament
Discharged filament

Undischarged nematocyst   Discharged nematocyst

THE STINGING THREAD
Under the microscope it is possible to see tiny sting-containing cells on the tentacles of coelenterate (cnidarian) animals. When the cell is triggered by touch or certain chemicals, its internal fluid pressure quickly increases. This forces the thread-like filament to shoot out. Some filaments are barbed; others contain venom.

PRAWN SNACK
This snakelocks anemone is in the process of capturing a common prawn and pulling it toward its mouth. The barbed stinging cells in the tentacles help to paralyze the prey. When the prawn is drawn into the anemone's stomach, more stings will finish it off.

MICROSCOPIC STINGERS
Hydroids such as these *Obelia* are tiny anemone-like creatures that grow in colonies. They form a furry coating on submerged seaweeds, rocks, and wood. Each individual has a stalk about as thick as cotton thread.

Green
snakelocks
anemone

Anemone ejects strings (acontia) of stinging cells from its mouth to defend itself

Stars of the sea

ON ALMOST ANY SEASHORE, somewhere, there will be sea stars - and probably a few of their relatives such as brittle stars, sea urchins, and sea cucumbers. These creatures belong to a group called the echinoderms (meaning "spiny skinned") and they have been around for perhaps 500 million years. Sea stars that are not spiny are protected by an exoskeleton (outer skeleton) of hard, chalky plates embedded just under the tough skin. Although there are more than 6,000 species of echinoderms - 2,000 more species than there are within the mammal group - these creatures are sea dwellers, so they are unfamiliar to most people. They also seem strange because their body plan consists of "arms" arranged like rays coming from a central point. There is no front end: when a sea star goes for a walk to follow the retreating tide or find a cool spot out of the sun, any arm can take the lead.

IN THE LIMELIGHT
Sunbeams shining through the surface of a tide pool spotlight shore sea stars. The "sausage with a frill" (upper right) is a sea cucumber. In this relative of the sea star, the arms are tentacles around the mouth end.

A THORNY PROBLEM
The crown-of-thorns sea star feeds on coral. From time to time its numbers increase dramatically, causing much damage in places like Australia's Great Barrier Reef. Whether this is a natural cycle or the result of pollution is not clear.

NEWLY ARMED
Sea stars can grow new arms. If an arm is crushed by a boulder or torn by a predator, it can be cast off and a new one grows. In fact, as long as most of the central disk is intact, one remaining arm can grow four new ones.

Light-sensitive tips of arms often turn up to "see" the way

Spiny sea star

SNAKING MOVEMENT
The brittle star throws its fragile arms into serpent-like shapes as it glides swiftly through a tide pool. The arms really are brittle and easily broken, but the brittle star is able to grow new ones.

Brittle star

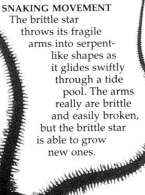

Blood star

SEEING RED
The blood star, seen occasionally on rocky shores, lives up to its other name of "bloody Henry" with its vivid red body marks.

MUSSEL POWER
This common sea star preys on mussels and other mollusks. It wraps itself around the victim, grips with its tube feet, gradually pulls open the two shells, and sticks out its stomach to digest the prey's soft parts.

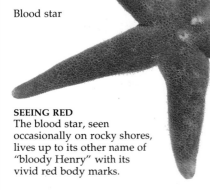

COVERED IN SPINES
Stiff and muscular, the spiny sea star is one of the larger sea-shore species. Each calcareous (chalky) spine is surrounded by tiny pincer-like organs (pedicellariae). It uses these to rid itself of parasites, small hitchhikers, and other debris. This sea star feeds on bivalve mollusks.

Spiny
sea star

LEFT STRANDED
Most sea stars live low on the shore or in deeper
water. Those washed up by stormy seas and
stranded out of the water may not survive until
the tide returns.

HUNGRY STARLETS
Small cushion stars, or "starlets," are as
carnivorous (meat-eating) as their larger
cousins, devouring little mollusks,
brittle stars, and
shore worms.

COMMONLY ORANGE
Many common sea stars are
orange, but some are brown,
red, or even purple.
Color variation is
frequent among
these creatures.

Goosefoot sea star
(right)

Spiny
sun star
(below)

WEBBED ARMS
Although the goosefoot sea star
(far right) looks like a five-sided
bandage, it is an active predator
and feeds on crustaceans, mollusks,
and other sea stars.

TWELVE-RAYED SUN
This spiny sun star (right) has
12 arms, but individuals with as
few as 8 or as many as 13 are not
unusual. Like the goosefoot
sea star, it will eat other
echinoderms such as
the common sea star.

Borers and builders

ON THE COAST OF CALIFORNIA in the late 1920s, steel girders and piles were installed for a seaside pier. About 20 years later, the .4 in (1 cm) thick steel was honeycombed with holes. The culprit was the purple sea urchin. This animal, like many others on the shore, takes refuge from waves, predators, sunshine, and cold by boring into the shore itself. Sand and mud, softer than solid rock, contain many burrowers, such as razor clams, cockles, clams, and tellins. (A razor clam is said to burrow as fast as a human can dig down after it.) Yet even on a rocky shore there are burrowers, boring, scraping, and dissolving their way into the rock. They include the piddock which, as it wears away the surface layer of its shell by drilling, moves its body over the worn area and lays down a fresh layer of hard, chalky shell. Pieces of wood riddled with long holes some .8 in (2 cm) across are often cast up on the beach. These are the work of shipworms, which despite their appearance are not worms but bivalve mollusks (p. 26), like piddocks.

HIDEY-HOLES IN THE ROCK
Rock-boring sea urchins have made many holes in this section of limestone coast at The Burren, in southwest Ireland. Unoccupied holes collect pebbles that are swirled around by the sea, scouring the rock still more. In these ways, rock-boring urchins and mollusks contribute to the erosion of the shore.

Date mussels in limestone

DISSOLVING STONE
The date mussel of the Mediterranean is one of several mollusks that can insert themselves into solid rock. Here two small specimens have bored into limestone. Instead of physically drilling into the rock like the piddock, these mussels secrete chemicals which dissolve the chalky stone. Their scientific name is *Lithophaga*, which means "eating rock." The growth rings typical of many bivalve mollusks are visible on the larger individual.

Growth ring

BUILDING A HOME
Several kinds of marine worms make tubes around themselves, chiefly to protect their soft bodies. *Terebella* (left) moves tiny particles with its tentacles and glues them together with a sticky body secretion. *Serpula* (center) makes a chalky, trumpet-shaped tube. Fan worms (right) make tubes that protrude above lower-shore sand.

TRIANGLE TUBES
Keelworms are another type of tube-building marine worm. Their chalky tubes have a "keel" or edge, so that they appear triangular in cross section. Their feathery tentacles collect tiny bits of food from seawater.

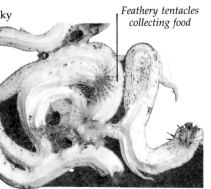
Feathery tentacles collecting food

Piddock in mudstone

PRISONER IN SOLID ROCK
The piddock's ridged shell resembles the sharply ribbed drilling bit of an oil rig, and not without reason. This mollusk twists and rocks the two parts (valves) of its shell in order to drill itself a hole in solid rock. Two long, fleshy tubes called siphons reach up through the hole. Seawater is drawn in through one tube to supply the animal with oxygen and food; waste and rock debris are passed out through the other.

GROW IN A BURROW
Several species of sea urchin are able to make shallow depressions in the rock, and some can burrow almost out of sight. The rock-boring or burrowing purple sea urchin moves its strong, stout spines back and forth and gradually rasps its way into the rock. It also grinds away the rock with its gnawing mouth-parts. As it grows and burrows, it may be unable to escape from its tunnel and becomes dependent on capturing food with its tube feet (p. 28).

Skeleton (test)

Urchins shelter in shallow "caves" excavated in rock

Spines are purple in life

ROCK RESIDENT
The purple sea urchin lives on the lower shore and in the shallows. Above the low-tide mark, it scrapes a shallow "home" in the rock.

Holes where sponge's breathing and feeding pores are exposed (p. 19)

Borings of yellow sponge

Shell of flat oyster

A BORING ANIMAL
The yellow boring sponge makes branching tunnels in limestone or in a thick, chalky seashell by dissolving the minerals with an acidic secretion. Small parts of the sponge project above each tunnel. They have either one large hole (pore) through which waste water passes out, or several smaller sieve-covered holes through which water is drawn in (p. 19).

Hard cases

SOME OF THE MOST CURIOUS LOOKING creatures of the shore are crabs, prawns, and lobsters. They are members of a large and varied group of animals called the crustaceans. In the same way that insects swarm on land, so crustaceans teem in the sea. Both groups are arthropods, or joint-legged animals. Crustaceans usually have jointed limbs (up to 17 pairs in some species), two pairs of antennae, and a hard shell, or carapace, that encloses and protects much of the body. However, the animals themselves vary enormously. They range from microscopic creatures that make up a large part of the floating plankton (the "soup" that nourishes so many filter-feeding sea animals), to the giant spider crabs of Japan, which measure more than 12 ft (3.5 m) across the claw tips. Some of the most surprising members of the crustacean group are the barnacles (cirripeds). These animals begin life as tiny, free-swimming larvae. Some species then settle on the shore, cement their "heads" to the rock, grow hard plates around their bodies, and use their six pairs of feathery, jointed "legs" to kick food into their mouths! The crustaceans most familiar to us are the decapods, which include shore creatures such as crabs, lobsters, crayfish, hermit crabs, prawns, and shrimps.

POTTED CRAB
Crabs have long been caught, cooked, and eaten by people. Crab pots are filled with rotting fish flesh as bait; once the crab has entered, it is unable to climb out. Crabs are also eaten by shore birds and mammals, by fish such as bass, and by octopuses.

Decapod means "10-legged," and most of these creatures have 10 main limbs. Four pairs are for walking or swimming, and there is one pair of handlike pincers.

The combative shore crab, pincers held up in self-defense, is known in France as *le crabe enragé*

BATTLE-SCARRED SCUTTLER
This shore crab has lost one of its limbs. A herring gull's powerful bill, or perhaps a small rock rolled by a wave, has removed its right first walking leg. Accidents like this often happen to crabs on rocky shores. However, this individual is not disabled by the loss and displays a variety of postures: caution (below), a mock attack, a crouching defense, and finally a retreat.

THE RED CARPET
In some areas of the Galápagos Islands off the coast of Ecuador, Sally Lightfoot crabs cover surf-splashed rocks like a moving red carpet. This brilliantly colored species has bright red limbs and a sky-blue underside.

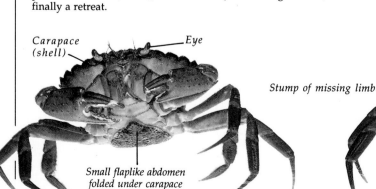

Carapace (shell)

Eye

Stump of missing limb

Four pairs of walking limbs

Small flaplike abdomen folded under carapace

Pincers poised in mock attack

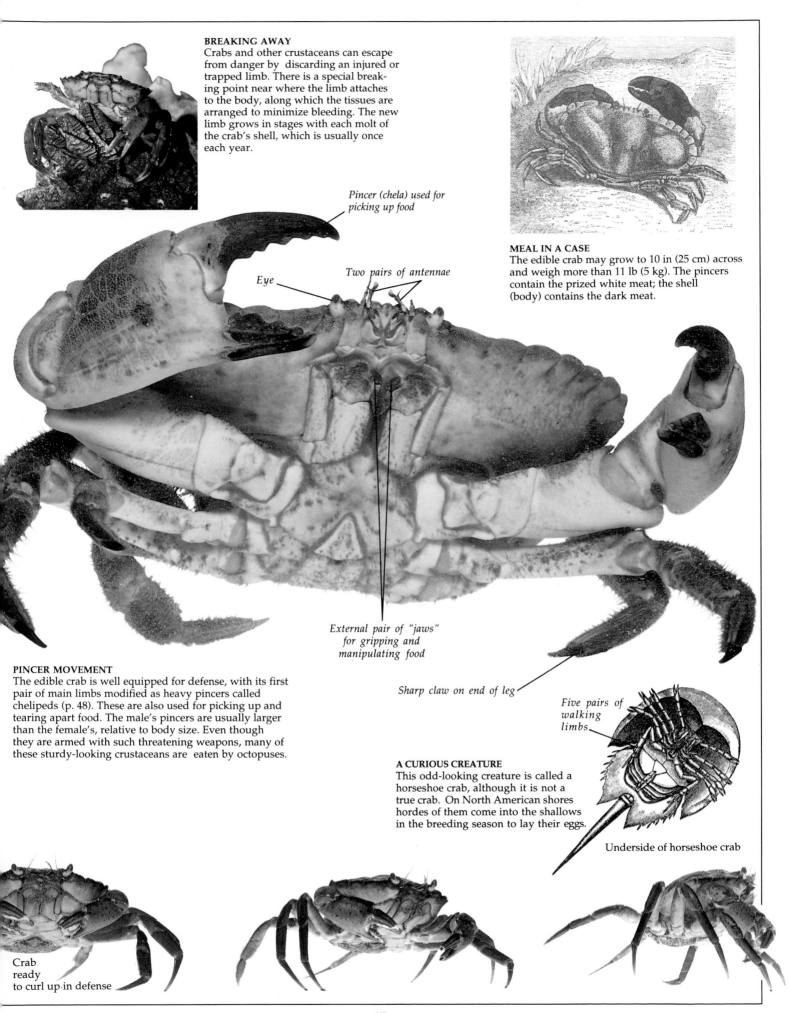

BREAKING AWAY
Crabs and other crustaceans can escape from danger by discarding an injured or trapped limb. There is a special breaking point near where the limb attaches to the body, along which the tissues are arranged to minimize bleeding. The new limb grows in stages with each molt of the crab's shell, which is usually once each year.

Pincer (chela) used for picking up food

Eye

Two pairs of antennae

MEAL IN A CASE
The edible crab may grow to 10 in (25 cm) across and weigh more than 11 lb (5 kg). The pincers contain the prized white meat; the shell (body) contains the dark meat.

External pair of "jaws" for gripping and manipulating food

PINCER MOVEMENT
The edible crab is well equipped for defense, with its first pair of main limbs modified as heavy pincers called chelipeds (p. 48). These are also used for picking up and tearing apart food. The male's pincers are usually larger than the female's, relative to body size. Even though they are armed with such threatening weapons, many of these sturdy-looking crustaceans are eaten by octopuses.

Sharp claw on end of leg

Five pairs of walking limbs

A CURIOUS CREATURE
This odd-looking creature is called a horseshoe crab, although it is not a true crab. On North American shores hordes of them come into the shallows in the breeding season to lay their eggs.

Underside of horseshoe crab

Crab ready to curl up in defense

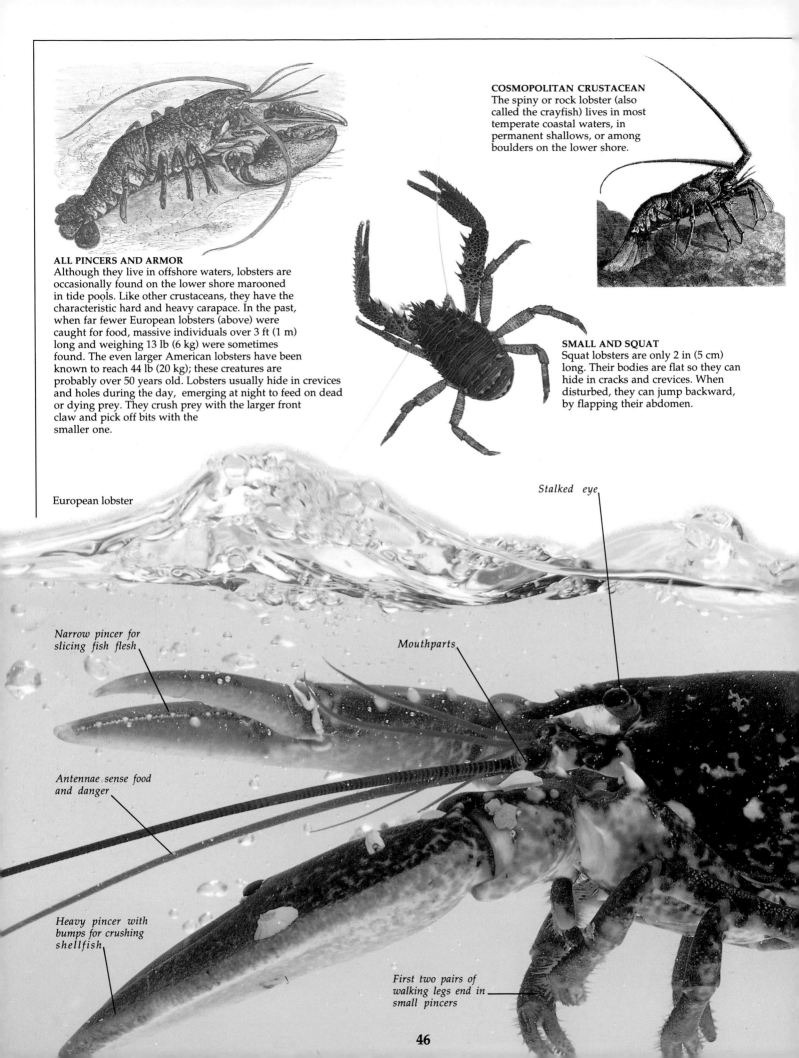

ALL PINCERS AND ARMOR
Although they live in offshore waters, lobsters are occasionally found on the lower shore marooned in tide pools. Like other crustaceans, they have the characteristic hard and heavy carapace. In the past, when far fewer European lobsters (above) were caught for food, massive individuals over 3 ft (1 m) long and weighing 13 lb (6 kg) were sometimes found. The even larger American lobsters have been known to reach 44 lb (20 kg); these creatures are probably over 50 years old. Lobsters usually hide in crevices and holes during the day, emerging at night to feed on dead or dying prey. They crush prey with the larger front claw and pick off bits with the smaller one.

COSMOPOLITAN CRUSTACEAN
The spiny or rock lobster (also called the crayfish) lives in most temperate coastal waters, in permanent shallows, or among boulders on the lower shore.

SMALL AND SQUAT
Squat lobsters are only 2 in (5 cm) long. Their bodies are flat so they can hide in cracks and crevices. When disturbed, they can jump backward, by flapping their abdomen.

European lobster

Stalked eye

Narrow pincer for slicing fish flesh

Mouthparts

Antennae sense food and danger

Heavy pincer with bumps for crushing shellfish

First two pairs of walking legs end in small pincers

NOT ONLY ROCK-BOTTOM
The coral crab lives in various habitats, frequenting rocky-bottomed shores, sandy areas, and sponges on coral reefs. It is found along the east coast of North America.

CRAB IN THE SKY
Early astronomers saw a crablike pattern of stars in the northern night sky and named it Cancer after the Latin word for a crab. Cancer is also the fourth sign of the zodiac, with the sun passing through from about June 21 to July 22.

A CLEANER COAST
Most crabs are adept scavengers, and the furrowed crab is no exception, picking up almost anything edible from the seabed. It lives around European coasts.

Barnacle cemented to lobster's body

Growth of bryozoans, a colony of tiny anemone-like animals (p. 25)

Tail fan helps to propel lobster backward when the tail is straightened and then suddenly flexed

Tail (abdomen)

Second two pairs of walking legs end in claws

Curly, protective tube of small marine worm

Swimmerets under tail enable lobster to bounce and swim as it moves along the bottom

Unusual partnerships

THERE ARE MANY TYPES of relationships in the animal world. A very familiar example is when one animal hunts and eats another. This is the predator-prey relationship. Yet nature is not always so cut and dried. On the seashore, as in other habitats, different kinds of animals are regularly seen together. This does not happen by chance - there is a reason. Scientists have different names for these relationships. In the relationship that is called parasitism, one partner, the parasite, benefits, but the other, the host, loses. Some shore crabs are host to *Sacculina*, a strange creature related to the barnacles. *Sacculina* attaches itself to a young crab and then grows "tentacles" that eat into the crab's body. This parasite gets food while disabling the crab. Another type of relationship, in which both partners benefit, is called symbiosis. The hermit crab and the calliactis anemone live in this way. The calliactis is sometimes called the parasitic anemone, but it does not harm its hermit host. It feeds on particles of food that the crab drops, and the crab is protected by the stinging tentacles.

HERMITS AT HOME
Hermit crabs do not have shells of their own, so they hide their soft bodies in the shells of dead animals. Sometimes an anemone is attached to the shell. As the crab grows and moves to a larger shell, it often takes the anemone along with it. There are also land hermit crabs in the tropics. Some species live in hollow mangrove roots or bamboo stems.

THREE-IN-ONE
Each of the three animals in this "partnership" comes from a different major animal group. The hermit crab is a crustacean (p. 44). The anemone is a coelenterate (cnidarian) (p. 36). The shell once belonged to a whelk, which is a sea snail and member of the mollusk group (p. 26).

STING IN THE PINCER
The boxer crab carries small anemones in its pincers. They act as "stinging clubs" and are waved at any creature posing a threat.

Keelworm tubes inside shell

CLAW IN THE DOOR
In its defensive position, the hermit crab pulls itself deep inside the shell. The right front claw (cheliped), which bears the large pincer, is usually bigger than the left one, and the crab holds it across the shell's entrance to make an effective door. (In this example the pincer is missing; it may have been bitten off by a predator or squashed by a boulder.)

SWEEPING THE FLOOR
The tentacles of anemones reach upward for floating or swimming victims. However, a calliactis anemone on a hermit crab's shell tends to hang down and sweep the rocks for bits of food "spilled" by the hermit crab.

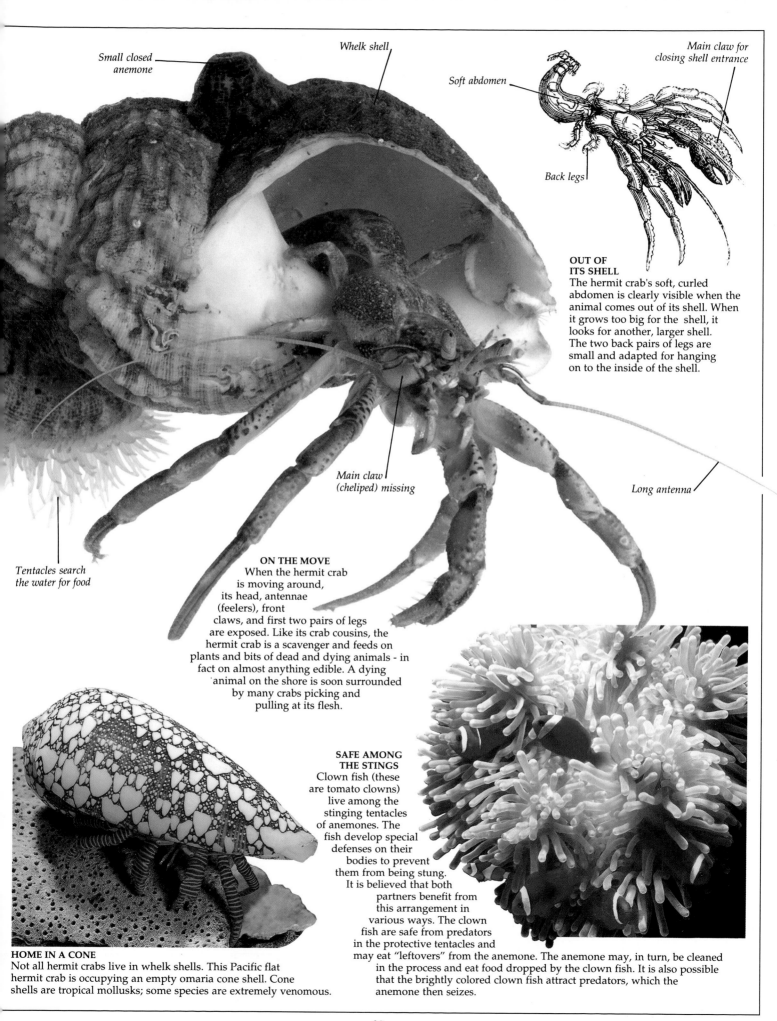

Small closed anemone

Whelk shell

Soft abdomen

Main claw for closing shell entrance

Back legs

OUT OF ITS SHELL

The hermit crab's soft, curled abdomen is clearly visible when the animal comes out of its shell. When it grows too big for the shell, it looks for another, larger shell. The two back pairs of legs are small and adapted for hanging on to the inside of the shell.

Main claw (cheliped) missing

Long antenna

Tentacles search the water for food

ON THE MOVE

When the hermit crab is moving around, its head, antennae (feelers), front claws, and first two pairs of legs are exposed. Like its crab cousins, the hermit crab is a scavenger and feeds on plants and bits of dead and dying animals - in fact on almost anything edible. A dying animal on the shore is soon surrounded by many crabs picking and pulling at its flesh.

SAFE AMONG THE STINGS

Clown fish (these are tomato clowns) live among the stinging tentacles of anemones. The fish develop special defenses on their bodies to prevent them from being stung. It is believed that both partners benefit from this arrangement in various ways. The clown fish are safe from predators in the protective tentacles and may eat "leftovers" from the anemone. The anemone may, in turn, be cleaned in the process and eat food dropped by the clown fish. It is also possible that the brightly colored clown fish attract predators, which the anemone then seizes.

HOME IN A CONE

Not all hermit crabs live in whelk shells. This Pacific flat hermit crab is occupying an empty omaria cone shell. Cone shells are tropical mollusks; some species are extremely venomous.

Disguises

A CASUAL GLANCE into a tide pool may reveal only a few strands of seaweed and some dead-looking shells. But wait patiently, sitting low and still to avoid being seen, and watch carefully. A dark patch of rock may suddenly glide forward: it is a blenny, on the look-out for food. A slightly hazy-looking area of sand walks away: it is a prawn adjusting the spots and lines on its body to blend perfectly with the background. A small pebble slides off: it is a periwinkle grazing on algae. A patch of gravelly bottom ripples and two eyes appear: a flatfish has tossed small pebbles and shell fragments over its body to break up its outline. All these creatures use camouflage to help conceal themselves. Looks are not everything, though - behavior is important too. The eel-like pipefish (p. 34) tends to swim in an upright position to blend in with the ribbons of seaweed and eelgrass in which it hides.

PALE UNDERSIDE
Flatfish are usually well camouflaged when viewed from the surface of the water. The underside, flat against the seabed, has no need of special coloring, so in many species it is white or pale.

LOOKING LIKE A WEED
The leafy sea dragon, from the coastal waters of southern Australia, is a type of sea horse. Its loose lobes of skin resemble the seaweed fronds in which it hides.

URCHIN COVER-UP
Several species of sea urchins grasp pebbles, shells, and pieces of seaweed with their long tube feet (p. 28) and hold them over their bodies. A well-draped urchin can be difficult to spot. These are green sea urchins, which are found on the lower shore and inshore waters.

DAB HAND AT CHANGE
Many flatfish can change their coloring to match the bottom on which they are resting. Some minutes earlier, this young dab was a light sandy color. It soon became several shades darker when placed on selected dark pebbles. The marks on its upper side became almost black. The largest dabs reach about 16 in (40 cm) long.

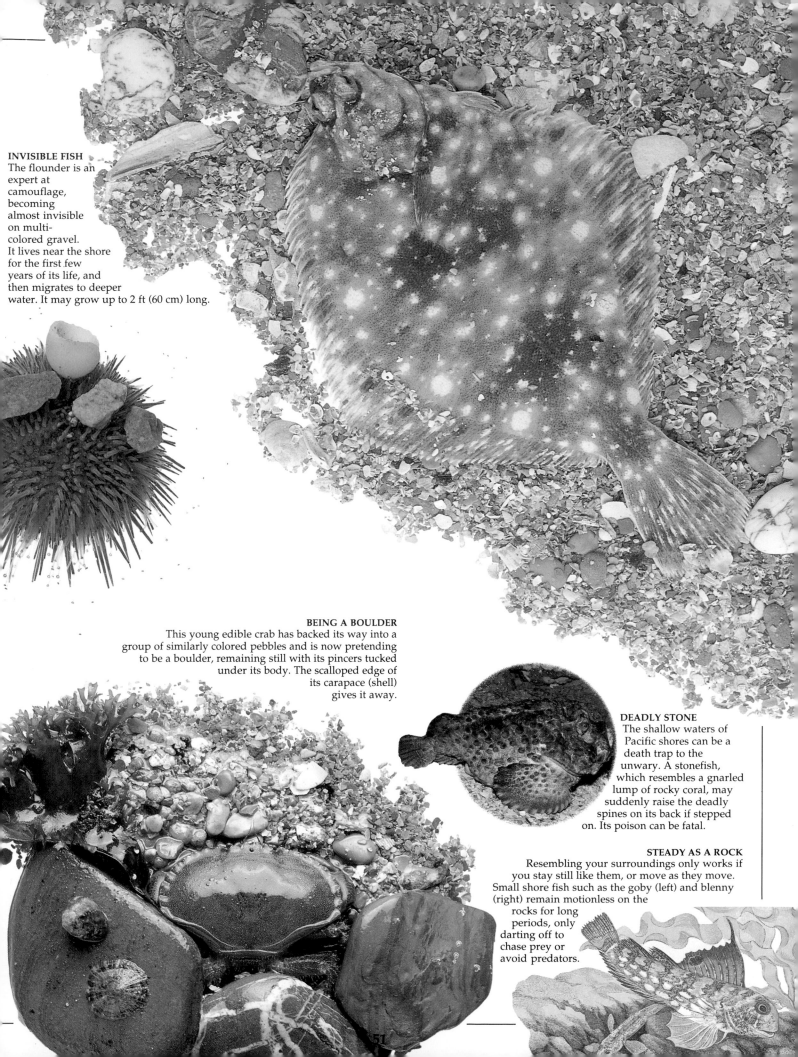

INVISIBLE FISH
The flounder is an expert at camouflage, becoming almost invisible on multi-colored gravel. It lives near the shore for the first few years of its life, and then migrates to deeper water. It may grow up to 2 ft (60 cm) long.

BEING A BOULDER
This young edible crab has backed its way into a group of similarly colored pebbles and is now pretending to be a boulder, remaining still with its pincers tucked under its body. The scalloped edge of its carapace (shell) gives it away.

DEADLY STONE
The shallow waters of Pacific shores can be a death trap to the unwary. A stonefish, which resembles a gnarled lump of rocky coral, may suddenly raise the deadly spines on its back if stepped on. Its poison can be fatal.

STEADY AS A ROCK
Resembling your surroundings only works if you stay still like them, or move as they move. Small shore fish such as the goby (left) and blenny (right) remain motionless on the rocks for long periods, only darting off to chase prey or avoid predators.

Life on a ledge

A SEABIRD BREEDING COLONY is one of the most spectacular sights on a rocky coastline. Coastal cliffs, rocky islets, and isolated islands can be reached only by flight and so make safe nesting places for birds. Here they are out of reach of all but the most agile ground-based predators, such as snakes and rats, and just beneath the waves there is a rich source of food. The sight of more than 50,000 gannets nesting on an offshore island is breathtaking. The impression is of a blizzard of large white birds coming and going, wheeling on their 6 ft (1.8 m) wings in currents of air, rising up the sheer cliff, regurgitating fish for their chicks, and screeching and pecking at any intruder - gannet or otherwise - that comes within reach of their spearlike bills.

EGG ON A ROCK
The razorbills of the Northern Hemisphere resemble their southern relatives, the penguins, although unlike penguins they are good fliers. On cliffs they form breeding colonies which may number tens of thousands of birds. Each female lays a single egg.

WARNING
All the eggs shown here come from a museum collection. (The colors have faded slightly.) Collecting or handling wild birds' eggs is now illegal.

EGGS DOWN A HOLE
Puffins nest in burrows. They dig their own holes in soft soil or take over an old shearwater or rabbit tunnel. Puffin eggs are white because, since they are hidden, they have no need of camouflage.

A puffin near a cliff-top burrow by the British bird artist Archibald Thorburn

An adult and a juvenile herring gull by Archibald Thorburn

SUITABLY SHAPED
The blotchy patterned egg of the guillemot is suitably shaped for life on a ledge, as it tapers narrowly to a point at one end. If it is blown around by the wind or kicked by the bird on the bare rock (the guillemot does not make a nest), it rolls around in a tight circle until it comes to rest.

FIERCE FEEDER
Herring gulls are noisy and aggressive. The squawks and screams coming from their nesting colonies are deafening. The average clutch consists of three eggs.

Common or great cormorant

Sharp, hooked bill for
holding on to slippery
prey

A NATURAL FERTILIZER
Guano, the accumulated droppings from a sea bird (or
bat) colony, is rich in nitrogen, potassium, and
phosphorus. Mining guano was a world trade in the last
century; most of it came from South American and African
coasts and islands, and was shipped to Europe
and North America for use as a fertilizer.

DRYING AFTER A DIP
Common or great cormorants are the largest of
the 29 species in the cormorant group and are
found almost worldwide. They swim and dive
after crabs, fish, and other aquatic prey.
Afterward they stand in a typical pose with
wings outstretched to dry them. Why cormorants
have not evolved water-repellent oils, like
many other sea birds, is a mystery.

Long flexible neck for
darting at victims

SHIFT WORK
Many cormorants nest by the sea on cliffs, rocky
ledges, and sloping stone slabs. Both cormorant
parents build their nest from sticks, seaweed, and
other locally gathered plant material. The parents
take turns incubating their three to five eggs
for about one month
until the chicks
hatch.

All four toes are webbed,
enabling the cormorant
to swim well

Feeding by the sea

FISH are wriggly, slippery creatures. Many animals that catch them have specially adapted mouths that can hang on to their awkward prey. Fish-eating mammals such as seals have many small, pointed teeth for this purpose. Fish-eating birds are generally equipped with long, sharp, dagger-like bills (beaks), and the bills of cormorants and many of the gulls also have a down-curved tip that prevents fish from slipping out of the end. Gulls are a familiar sight along the coasts of the Northern Hemisphere. They hunt along the shore, catching tide-pool fish, pecking at crabs, and hammering open shellfish. Like many other sea birds, they tend to feed near land during the breeding season, but then wander off to lead a mostly pelagic (open-ocean) life for the rest of the year.

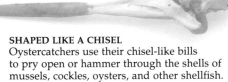

AN ALL-PURPOSE BILL
Herring gulls have broad bills, capable of handling all kinds of prey including the contents of rubbish dumps.

SHAPED LIKE A CHISEL
Oystercatchers use their chisel-like bills to pry open or hammer through the shells of mussels, cockles, oysters, and other shellfish.

SPEARED FROM ABOVE
The gannet dives from as high as 100 ft (30 m) to catch herring, sardines, mackerel, and other fish. This bird also uses its bill to fight enemies and to stab at those who intrude into its nesting space.

Tubelike nostrils

A HOOKED BILL
Fulmars nest in groups on rocky islands and cliffs. They feed on surface-dwelling fish and their beaks are hooked at the end. They have prominent tubelike nostrils lying along the top or sides of the bill.

Small wings are used as paddles in the water, and flap rapidly in flight

DANGEROUS WORK
Sea birds and their eggs are still caught and eaten along some remote shores. On the island of St. Kilda, off the northwest coast of Scotland, this practice continued until the 1940s. Birds flying past an outcrop were caught in a net; eggs and nestlings were collected by hand. Gannets, fulmars (right), and various auks were the main victims.

FISHERMAN'S FRIEND
For centuries, coastal people in eastern Asia have fished with trained cormorants. A collar and lead is put on the bird so that it can catch fish but not swallow them. The bird is then pulled back to the boat by the lead. Today this "fishing" has become a tourist attraction.

A BILL FULL OF EELS
After a diving session, a catch of up to 10 small fish (such as these sand eels) is not unusual for the stripe-billed puffin. This bird lives throughout the North Atlantic.

GOOD FOR SWIMMING
The guillemot or murre (p. 52) has relatively large, powerful feet with strong webs. Its legs are positioned far back along its body so that it swims efficiently, but on land it waddles rather than walks, with an upright, penguin-like stance.

Guillemot often rests on "heels" (shanks) on a ledge, rather than standing

SWOOPING ON THE SHORE
It is thought that the gull's pale underside matches the sky or clouds, making this bird less visible to fish, crabs, and other prey as they look up, on the watch for danger. This is a young herring gull with mottled plumage. Adult birds have white bellies.

Claw-tipped toes

UNDERWATER PROPELLERS
The gannet's great webbed feet can propel the bird at remarkable speed under the water as it chases after fish. It also uses its feet to cover and help incubate the egg.

During the breeding season, the egg (p. 52) is balanced on the large, webbed feet

Visitors to the shore

NOW AND AGAIN, we may be lucky enough to see some of the larger visitors to the shore. Marine turtles crawl onto land under cover of darkness to lay their eggs in the warm sand. Seals sunbathe, and sometimes the bulls (males) fight each other for the right to mate with a harem of females. In the Arctic, white-tusked walruses lie in steaming heaps on the icy rock; near the Equator, marine iguana lizards crop seaweeds from the rocky shores of the Galápagos Islands. In Antarctica, penguins gather by the millions to rest and breed. However, some visitors to the shore come by accident. The strandings of schools of live whales have long puzzled scientists.

SUN, SEA, AND SAND
During the last century the seaside became popular with one mammal in particular. As is usual with this species, it has greatly changed the habitat. Nowadays, beaches are crowded with its family groups, while the inshore waters are congested with its brightly colored toys, such as yachts and windsurfing boards.

LARDER WITH FLIPPERS
The green turtle, the only plant eater among the six species of sea turtles, travels across the world's tropical oceans. Females come ashore to lay eggs in shallow holes in the sand. They tend to use the same breeding places, or rookeries, year after year - making it easy for hunters to capture them and steal their eggs. This species grows to 3 ft (1 m) long and 400 lb (180 kg) in weight. It is sometimes called the edible turtle, and in former times it was hunted mercilessly for its flesh, oil, skin, and shell. Today it is officially listed as an endangered species.

STRANDED SQUID
Giant squid, voracious deep-sea predators, are occasionally washed up on the shore. Such stranded individuals are probably injured, ill, or already dead when swept in by shore-bound currents. Giant squid are the largest of all invertebrate animals (those without backbones). They grow to more than 50 ft (15 m) in total length and weigh up to 2 tons.

THE CRADLE OF THE SHALLOWS
The sea otter lives off the coasts of the Pacific Ocean and rarely comes ashore, preferring to lie in the calm of a kelp bed (p. 22). It feeds on sea urchins, crustaceans, and shellfish, and will use a stone as a tool to crush the hard shells of its prey. This is the heaviest of the 12 otter species, sometimes weighing as much as 100 lb (45 kg). The sea otter became extremely rare, as it was hunted for its fur, but in 1911 an international agreement (one of the first of its kind) rescued it from extinction.

LIFE ON THE OCEAN WAVE
Harbor seal pups (these are about three months old) are born on land, but they can swim and dive almost immediately after birth. Seals haul themselves out of the water to bask on rocks and sandbanks, or to give birth. Harbor seals live in coastal waters in the North Pacific and North Atlantic. Recently a viral illness has killed many thousands of those living in the North Sea.

Beachcombing

Twice each day the sea rises up the shore and then retreats, depositing debris along the high-tide mark. This is the strandline, a ribbon of objects left stranded high and dry. It is a treasure trove for the nature detective. Shells, bits of seaweed, feathers, and driftwood lie jumbled together, each with a story to tell. Stones, shells, and wood have often been smoothed and sculpted by the sea, rolled back and forth in the sand or crashed against the rocks and split open. Seaweeds torn from rocks are carried along in currents and washed up farther along the coast. Large-scale ocean currents such as the Gulf Stream can transport floating objects thousands of miles and dump them on some distant shore.

Certain plants use the sea to spread their seeds; the coconut is a famous example. The familiar nut itself ripens inside an even larger husk of stringy gray fibers (the coir, which is woven into rough mats and ropes) encased in a brownish leathery skin. This makes a fine "float" and, when a coastal coconut palm drops a husk almost straight into the ocean, it is carried by currents and deposited on a distant shore, where it may grow. In this way coconut palms have spread to fringe tropical shores around the world.

A PEACEFUL PASTIME
Beachcombing is rewarding, as almost anything may be washed up on the shore. In the past people made a living by collecting and selling curios, food, and other objects found on the shore. Today not all shores are suitable for beachcombing, as many are strewn with man-made litter, and inshore waters are often polluted.

FOOD FOR FREE
Many seaweeds are gathered as food for both humans and animals (p. 23) and for use as fertilizers. Algae such as carrageen are rich in nutrients. For some coastal peoples they are a good source of trace elements - minerals that the human body needs in small quantities. Seaweed also has medical applications: recently a jelly-like seaweed extract used as a lining for bandages for burns has been found to be very effective.

DRIED FLOAT
Rockweed, which grows in large quantities on sheltered rocky shores, becomes green-black when dry. It has large air bladders which enable the weed to float at high tide.

Air bladder

DEAD HANDS
Dead-man's fingers is a common name given to a variety of sponges, soft corals, and bryozoans . These primitive animals (p. 19) tend to live off-shore and only the spongy, rubbery skeletons are cast up on the beach. Small animals and fish often find hiding places in the tunnel-ridden remains.

A 19th-century engraving entitled *Common objects at the sea-side...*

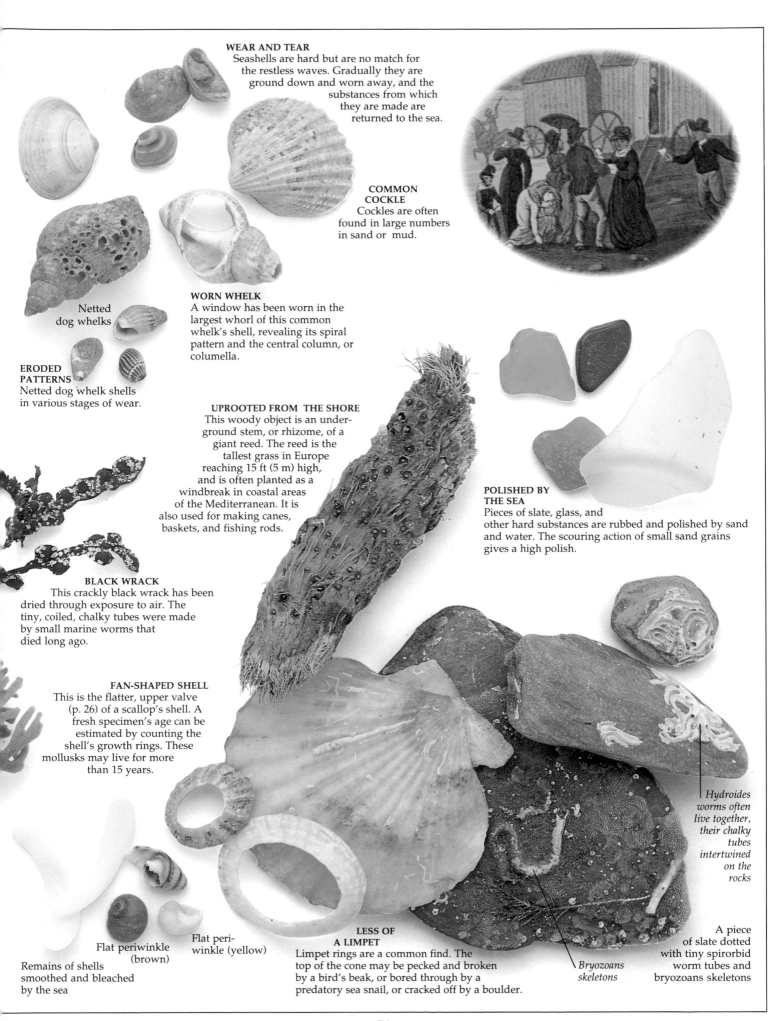

WEAR AND TEAR

Seashells are hard but are no match for the restless waves. Gradually they are ground down and worn away, and the substances from which they are made are returned to the sea.

COMMON COCKLE

Cockles are often found in large numbers in sand or mud.

WORN WHELK

A window has been worn in the largest whorl of this common whelk's shell, revealing its spiral pattern and the central column, or columella.

Netted dog whelks

ERODED PATTERNS

Netted dog whelk shells in various stages of wear.

UPROOTED FROM THE SHORE

This woody object is an underground stem, or rhizome, of a giant reed. The reed is the tallest grass in Europe reaching 15 ft (5 m) high, and is often planted as a windbreak in coastal areas of the Mediterranean. It is also used for making canes, baskets, and fishing rods.

POLISHED BY THE SEA

Pieces of slate, glass, and other hard substances are rubbed and polished by sand and water. The scouring action of small sand grains gives a high polish.

BLACK WRACK

This crackly black wrack has been dried through exposure to air. The tiny, coiled, chalky tubes were made by small marine worms that died long ago.

FAN-SHAPED SHELL

This is the flatter, upper valve (p. 26) of a scallop's shell. A fresh specimen's age can be estimated by counting the shell's growth rings. These mollusks may live for more than 15 years.

Hydroides worms often live together, their chalky tubes intertwined on the rocks

Flat periwinkle (brown)

Flat periwinkle (yellow)

LESS OF A LIMPET

Limpet rings are a common find. The top of the cone may be pecked and broken by a bird's beak, or bored through by a predatory sea snail, or cracked off by a boulder.

Remains of shells smoothed and bleached by the sea

Bryozoans skeletons

A piece of slate dotted with tiny spirorbid worm tubes and bryozoans skeletons

"Arms" of sea urchin

Test of edible sea urchin

Recently dead sea
urchin with some
spines still attached

Hole where
the anus
was in life

Neck

**HOLE IN
A STONE**
This stone was
formed around
an animal, the
traces of which
have long since
disappeared.

Hole where the
mouthparts were
in life

HOLES IN THE GLOBE
The sea urchin's hard, ball-shaped
skeleton is called a test (p. 28). The
pattern of bumps, hollows, and tiny holes held the spines and
tube feet in life, and the large hole contained the anus. Stripped
of its spines, the five-rayed symmetry (evenness) of the animal can be
seen, indicating this creature's relationship to the sea stars in the
echinoderm group. Urchins have been called sea stars with "arms"
held together over their heads. All the major body organs were
enclosed in and protected by the test. They included the gonads
(reproductive parts) and the roe (eggs or sperm), which people
in some areas collect and eat.

Broad, flat
rear limbs
for swimming

Broken parts
of ribs

A FISHY FIND
The skeletons of
bony fish such as
cod and bass are
sometimes cast up
on the shore. This
incomplete example
of a fish shows the rear
of the skull and the ver-
tebrae, or backbones, of the
neck and main body. These
sorts of remains may be the
work of fishermen who throw
young fish back into the sea.

Characteristic red
joints found on
the limbs of
this species

Top of carapace detached

Gills

A gull colony: a mass of noise,
droppings, and feathers

Space in
center occupied
by heart

A FEATHERY FIND
Sea bird feathers litter almost
every shore; they float like
corks and are easily blown
onto land by the wind. Some
are from dead birds, but many
are simply lost during the normal
plumage molt.

FALLING APART AT THE SEAMS
A velvet swimming crab in the early stages of
decay has fallen apart at the seams to reveal
its internal anatomy. The main organs are
contained in the central part of the body.
Two large chambers on either side house
the gills, with which this crustacean
absorbs the oxygen dissolved in
seawater.

Muscle (meat) in pincer already
partly eaten by scavengers

ALL WASHED UP
Pine cones and other light, woody objects may wash up on the seashore after floating down a small stream into a river and then into the sea.

Mature gull's wing feather

Barred feather typical of young gull

WIND POWER
An onshore wind tends to blow floating items toward the land, improving the beachcomber's chances of finding unusual things.

Cast-up and dried-out young dogfish

Shark in the shallows

The lesser-spotted dogfish, often simply called the dogfish, is a type of shark. It is harmless and grows to about 3 ft (1 m) in length. Dogfish spend most of their lives offshore, in water around 100-325 ft (30-100 m) deep. However, in late autumn, winter, and spring, females swim into shallow water near the shore to lay their eggs among seaweed.

OUT OF THE CASE
A newly hatched dogfish is about 4 in (10 cm) long. It usually still has part of the yolk sac attached, but this shrivels as the youngster begins to feed for itself. As an adult, it will hunt bottom-dwelling creatures such as shellfish.

BUNDLE OF EGGS
Empty egg cases of the whelk are another common beachcombing find. They are fixed to stones when laid, and tiny but fully formed young whelks crawl out of the cases.

WATER BABIES
The baby dogfish develop inside their egg cases, each nourished by its yolk sac. They continue to grow for up to 10 months before hatching.

THE MAGIC PURSE
The dogfish egg case is tied to anchoring weed by long tendrils at each corner. Empty cases are often washed up on the shore and are called mermaid's purses.

Studying our shores

We ENJOY OUR SEASHORES in many different ways. Children paddle in the ripples, surfers ride the waves, naturalists study plants and animals, local people collect seaweed and shellfish for food, and anyone may appreciate the beauty of unspoiled stretches of shore. However, our seashores are being damaged by the increasing pollution of the sea. Throughout history, scientists and researchers have studied our shorelines to understand the way nature works and the way nature is changing. Here we look at some of the tools that have been used in the past and today to help determine the health of our coastlines. We examine the effects of pollution in depth on pages 66–67.

POLLUTION INDICATORS
Some types of seaweeds react quickly to pollution and are termed "indicator species." Records of preserved seashore plants, combined with population surveys of shore inhabitants, help scientists monitor changes over time.

DIVING IN A GARBAGE CAN
In the 1930s the first scientific surveys of life in the permanent shallows were made. The scientists wore primitive diving hoods. Air was provided by two car pumps operated from the shore, and each hood contained a radio telephone.

SHELL SHOCK
Shell surveys show how the numbers of some species have been reduced by pollution or overfishing.

A CLOSER LOOK
The naturalist's invaluable magnifying lens needs a corrosion-proof frame and handle for seashore work.

SIFTING THROUGH THE SAND
Shrimps, cockles, and other edible shore creatures can be caught along the surf line in wet sand with a strong net. The wooden leading edge is pushed just below the surface; sand grains pass easily through the net, but larger objects are trapped. Shrimping was once a popular pastime as well as a commercial industry. But today many beaches have been overexploited, or are too polluted or too disturbed by vacationers to yield worthwhile catches.

TIDE GUIDE
Tide tables are essential for anyone who leaves the main beach to study rocks or flats. The tables give relative water heights as well as dates and times of low and high water. Most of the shore is exposed at the lowest spring tide.

ROCK RECORD
For scientific studies of the shoreline, a geological map is very important. Different types of rocks are color-coded, and height contours are given as on ordinary maps. Granite, sandstone, and similar hard rocks tend to form stable rocky shores; soft rocks like chalk and limestone are eroded more quickly.

ARTIST'S INSPIRATION
Many people are fascinated by the sea. They are in awe of its destructive power and attracted by its constant motion and sudden changes of mood. Artists have been inspired to sketch and paint hundreds of beach scenes, from tranquil summer afternoons to ferocious winter storms.

Waterproof flashlight

WATERPROOF EQUIPMENT
Modern waterproof cameras allow us to record nature without harming it. An underwater flashlight is another useful piece of equipment. Many larger animals, such as lobsters and crabs, hide themselves in caves and crevices on the cool, shadowy side of rocks. It is always a good idea to shine a light before putting in a hand, just in case!

LIFE IN THE BALANCE
We cannot see any of the dissolved chemicals in seawater, but their levels mean life or death for all sea creatures. Testing kits reveal amounts of substances, such as nitrites and nitrates, that indicate the degree of pollution present in the seawater. Large amounts of fertilizers, which contain nitrogen, are washed into the sea by rivers carrying soil eroded from the land. The hydrometer measures the density or "heaviness" of the seawater, which reveals the concentration of dissolved salts.

STUDYING SHORE LIFE
One way of studying the zonation of life on the shore (pp. 12-15) is to stretch a piece of string down to the sea's edge, if possible from the high-tide strandline to the low-tide mark. Begin at low tide, and move up the string, recording the commonest types of seaweeds and creatures at each stage. Don't forget: after an hour or so, the tide will start to return.

LIMPET LEVER
When examining snails and limpets, a knife helps to pry them gently from the rock. Always put them back in the same place.

NEVER USE A JACKNIFE WITHOUT AN ADULT TO HELP YOU

FASHION OF THE TIME
Fashionable bathing suits of the 19th century may seem rather quaint today. But how will today's suits be regarded a century from now?

OUT OF THEIR ELEMENT
Keep shore creatures only for essential study. They are out of their element: would you like to be dragged into the sea for an hour?

Did you know?

AMAZING FACTS

 There are around 40,000 species of crustaceans on Earth.

The biggest bivalve mollusk is the giant clam (*Tridacna gigas*), which is native to the Indo-Pacific Ocean and reaches a weight of around 496 lb (225 kg).

A lobster's blood is colorless. When exposed to oxygen, it develops a bluish color.

In just one spawning, a shrimp can produce about 500,000 eggs.

Seals swim at an average speed of 12 mph (19 k/ph). Humans swim at less than 1 mph (1.6 k/ph).

The tallest wave ever recorded in the open ocean reached a height of 112 ft (34 m). The wave was recorded by the team of the USS *Ramapo* in the Pacific Ocean in 1933. Tidal waves are produced by earthquakes and can often reach 33 ft (10 m) in height.

Sally-lightfoot crabs in the Galapagos

Sally-lightfoot crabs do not like being in the water. If forced into the water, they will run across the surface and get out at the first opportunity.

The sea-dwelling snails of the cone shell family include some highly deadly members. Found in tropical regions, these snails carry a poison that is injected by a radula, a mouthpart shaped like a harpoon. This poison can kill a human.

Pea crabs live inside oyster shells and eat food collected by the oyster. Pea crabs damage an oyster's body and are parasites, creatures that live off another living thing without giving anything back.

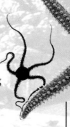

Sea star

Sea grasses are the only flowering plants in the sea. They are very important in coastal marine areas, as they are the main diet of dugong and green turtles and provide a habitat for many small marine animals. They also help to gather sediment, (floating particles of mud and soil) and so help to keep the water clear. Australia has the highest number of sea-grass species of any continent.

It takes an average of seven years for a lobster to grow by just 1 lb (0.45 kg) in weight.

Oysters can change from one gender to another and back again, depending on which is best for attracting a mate at that point in time.

Seals are capable of remaining underwater for up to 30 minutes, although they tend to surface after five minutes.

Sea stars are the only animals that can turn their stomachs inside out. Some sea stars can split their bodies in half and grow new legs to make two whole sea stars.

Puffins are incredible divers and can reach depths of 197 ft (60 m) to catch fish. They use their wings to propel themselves underwater and can carry several fish at a time back to the surface.

Climate change experts predict that sea levels may rise by up to 19.5 in (50 cm), by the year 2100, which will increase flooding and coastal erosion.

Waves pick up height and speed from wind.

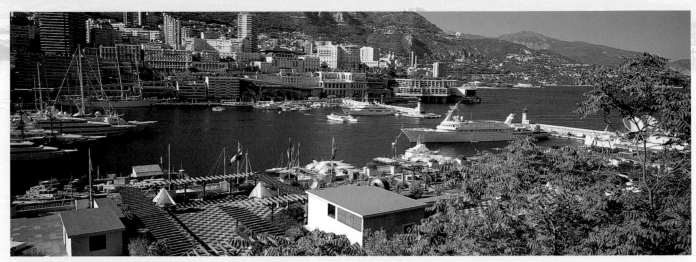

Monaco's coastline is heavily developed.

Q **Which country has the shortest coastline?**

A At just 3.5 miles (5.6 km), Monaco has the shortest coastline of any country. Not surprisingly, as the world's second largest country, Canada has the longest coastline, at 56,487 miles (90,908 km).

Q **Is it possible to purify shellfish from sewage-polluted water for safe eating?**

A Yes. If shellfish are transplanted from sewage-polluted water to clean water, they have the ability to purify themselves rapidly and so become safe to eat.

Record Breakers

HIGHEST TIDES
• Tides in the Bay of Fundy, Canada, can reach heights of more than 49 ft (15 m).

LARGEST CORAL REEF
• The Great Barrier Reef stretches for 1,260 miles (2,028 km) along the coast of Queensland in northeastern Australia. It covers twice the area of Iceland.

MOST VENOMOUS GASTROPOD
• The most venomous gastropod is the geographer cone shell, found in the Pacific.

BIGGEST CRUSTACEAN
• The Alaskan king crab is the largest crustacean, weighing up to 15 lb (6.7 kg) and measuring around 5 ft (1.5 m) across shell and claws.

LARGEST SEA TURTLE
• The leatherback is the largest of all sea turtles. It can weigh up to 1,404 lb (637 kg) and attain a length of 6 ft (1.85 m).

SALTIEST WATER
• The Red Sea has the saltiest seawater on Earth.

Q **What sea creatures are most dangerous to swimmers?**

A In some parts of the world, sharks pose the main threat to swimmers. Other sea creatures to be avoided include, barracudas, moray eels, octopuses, sharp-spined sea urchins, stingrays, toadfish, catfish, and jellyfish. The Portuguese man-of-war has tentacles that can reach 49 ft (15 m) and carry stings that produce painful welts on the human body.

Q **How did European ponies end up on the U.S. island of Assateague?**

A There is mystery surrounding how the population of wild ponies came to be on Assateague island, off Maryland and Virginia. The recent discovery of a sunken shipwreck near the island has supported the theory that a Spanish ship with a cargo of horses sank off the coast in the 1600s. Some horses swam ashore and have continued to breed through the years. There is now a robust population of around 300.

Wild ponies on Assateague Island

Q **How do oysters produce pearls?**

A A pearl begins when a foreign substance, such as a grain of sand, enters an oyster shell. The oyster's body reacts by depositing material around the foreign body to wall it off and reduce irritation. Over the years these deposits build up to create a pearl.

Q **Where do sea turtles breed?**

A Sea turtles live most of their lives in the ocean, but nesting females return to the beach where they were born. They must often travel very long distances from their feeding grounds to lay their eggs.

Q **Do fish ever sleep?**

A Fish do not sleep in the same way as humans, but they do rest. Fish cannot close their eyes, and some fish never stop moving. However, most fish have rest periods when they just float or nest in a quiet spot, while remaining semi-alert.

Protecting our coastlines

POLLUTION OF THE WORLD'S COASTLINES is an increasing threat to the animals and plants that live on the shore. Here we examine some of the effects of coastal pollution. We also look at some of the types of coastline that exist as a reminder of the delicate beauty that needs to be preserved. You can help protect seashore wildlife. As a visitor to the beach, always take your waste away and try to not disturb plants and animals. Find out if there are local volunteer programs that you can join, or start a research project at your school.

TOURISM
The Mediterranean sea turtle is under threat. These turtles need access to quiet beaches on which to lay their eggs, but many beaches have been overrun by tourism. Conservation projects, such as the one shown above, help to save turtles.

Discharge of sewage off the Mediterranean coast

SEWAGE WASTE
Around the world millions of tons of sewage and industrial waste are discharged into the oceans every day. Sewage and chemicals affect aquatic habitats and poison plant and animal life, also making the seas unsafe for humans to swim in.

OVERFISHING
In most parts of the world the rate of commercial fishing is so high that fish populations are not being given a chance to breed and maintain their numbers. The levels of most species of marine fish are at an all-time low.

OIL SPILLS
When ships carrying oil suffer a spill, the effects for a marine ecosystem are disastrous. Birds, fish, and plants that come into contact with the oil will be poisoned and often perish. These puffins were contaminated by an oil slick and died.

Nets can trap other fish as well as the intended catch.

A haul of salmon

SEA TRAFFIC
Development along coastlines, such as at ports, can wipe out natural habitats. Even without accidents, normal ship operations discharge a great deal of oil into the sea. Salerno in Italy, shown here, is divided into a fishing port and a tourist port, both of which have hundreds of ships coming and going daily.

BEACH POLLUTION
As inexpensive vacations and traveling become more popular, so are the world's beaches being slowly ruined. Sunbathers leave plastic bottles and other waste on the beach. Applied sunscreens also wash off in the water and build up chemical residues.

SHORELINE HABITATS

SHINGLE
A shingle beach is made up of pebbles or stones. This is one of the least hospitable beach habitats, as most plants and animals find it difficult to survive the constant disruption of the stones being moved by the tides. This shingle is from the Sussex coast in England.

BASALT
A basalt or black sand beach is made up of volcanic lava that has been broken down into fine grains by the waves over the years. This type of beach is quite rare, but there are stunning examples around the world, such as this one in Iceland.

White sand beach, Tanzania

ROCKY SHORE
Rocky shores are made up of rock pools, boulder fields, and flat rock platforms. A great diversity of plant and animal life thrives on these shores. Rock pools are mini–marine ecosystems, boulders offer shelter from weather, and platforms are home to species that need to stay dry. The shore above is in the Canadian Arctic.

WHITE SAND
This is the most popular type of beach for vacationers. White sand is rock, shells, or coral that have been ground into very fine particles and bleached by hot sun. Soft sand makes a welcoming home for burrowing animals and insects, and also allows predators easy access to them for food.

Find out more

Every shoreline is abundant with plant and animal life for you to discover. Just by walking along the beach, you will come across plenty of interesting specimens. Explore shallow waters or tide pools with a net. Beyond the beach, cliffs, caves, sand dunes, and salt marshes are home to many more plants and creatures. To learn about shore life in different parts of the world, visit a marine aquarium or a natural history museum.

SNORKELING
One of the best ways to find out about the plants and creatures that live on the shoreline is to go snorkeling. Accompanied by an adult, choose a rock-free stretch of water to swim in. Watch for fish, coral, plants, and pretty shells.

USEFUL WEB SITES

- Explore life in the Oceans of the world:
  www.seasky.org/sea.html
- Get a close look at the creatures that roam the ocean's depths. Learn about fish, mammals, and plant life:
  www.pbs.org/oceanrealm/seadwellers
- Find out how to identify, clean, and care for shells:
  www.seashells.org
- Kids Do Ecology presents Marine Mammal Pages:
  www.nceas.ucsb.edu/nceas-web/kids/mmp/home.htm

Mask and snorkel allow you to see and breathe face down in the water.

Places to Visit

SHEDD AQUARIUM, CHICAGO, IL
Exhibitions include Caribbean coral reefs, the Amazon, and pacific rocky coasts.

AQUARIUM OF THE AMERICAS, NEW ORLEANS, LA
Discover the creatures of North and South America underwater in the Aquarium's 30-foot-long aquatic tunnel surrounded by 132,000 gallons of water.

NATIONAL AQUARIUM, BALTIMORE, MD
A darkened shark exhibit allows close inspection with large sharks such as Sand tiger and nurse sharks.

NEW YORK AQUARIUM, BROOKLYN, NY
The aquarium offers a look at over 8,000 animals that include jellyfish in the new Alien Stingers exhibit, walruses in the Sea Cliffs exhibit, and sea lions in an Aquatheater presentation.

SEA WORLD, SAN ANTONIO, TX
Touch and feed bottle-nosed dolphins, see animal shows, and go on water rides at the world's largest marine-life adventure park.

MARINE AQUARIUM
Many cities have a marine aquarium that is home to hundreds of amazing sea creatures from around the world. During your visit, find out which plants and creatures stay far out at sea and which can be found living near the shoreline.

BEACHCOMBING

Any stroll along the shore will reveal an array of plants and creatures washed up by the tide. Look for shells, seaweed, jellyfish, and coral. Insects and burrowing creatures will be teeming just beneath the surface of any sandy beach. Close to rocks, you may find scuttling crabs and clinging shellfish.

TIDE POOLING

The best time to explore tide pools is at low tide, which happens twice a day. You can find out times by looking at tide tables and asking locally. Take a net to help you catch your finds and a plastic container or bucket to temporarily hold them. You may discover crabs, fish, seaweed, sea stars, and much more.

PLANT DISCOVERY

Coastal plants must be hardy to survive the extreme weather conditions that occur on exposed land. Salt marshes that form on lowlands behind the shore can be home to an array of sea grasses and rushes. Flowering plants are often found in sheltered spots.

BIRD WATCHING

There are many types of fascinating birds to be studied on the coast. Along with the ever-present gulls, you will see waders probing in the sand for food with their long beaks during low tides. Many birds make their nests on the cliffs, where they are relatively safe from humans and predators.

Glossary

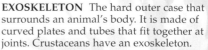

A crab is a crustacean.

ANTENNAE The sensory organs on each side of the head, also called feelers or horns. Antennae can have many functions, including, navigation, taste, sight, and hearing. Crabs, lobsters, and shrimp all have antennae.

ARTHROPOD A member of a major division of the animal kingdom with a segmented body and joined appendages (limbs), such as a crustacean or an insect

BIVALVE An animal with a shell in two parts or valves, such as an oyster or mussel

CALCAREOUS A substance containing or composed of calcium carbonate, such as chalk or limestone. Cliffs are often calcareous.

CAMOUFLAGE The means by which an animal escapes the notice of predators, usually because it blends in with its surroundings

CARAPACE The hard shield that covers the bodies of crabs, lobsters, and shrimp. The top part of a turtle's shell is also called a carapace.

CHELIPED The claw-bearing appendage (limb) of a crustacean

CHLOROPHYLL The green pigment present in most plants and central to photosynthesis, a process in which plants use sunlight to create their own food

COELENTERATE A water-dwelling invertebrate, usually with a simple tube-shaped body. Jellyfish, corals, and sea anemones are all coelenterates, or cnidarians.

Tropical fish can only live in a warm habitat.

CORAL A small sea animal that catches food with stinging tentacles. Many corals live in large colonies called coral reefs.

CORRASION The grinding up of the Earth's surface when rock particles are carried over it by pounding waves

CRUSTACEAN An invertebrate with jointed legs and two pairs of antennae

DORSAL FIN The fin located at the back or rear of a fish's body

ECOLOGY The study of the relationship between living things and their environment

ECHINODERM A sea animal with an internal skeleton and a body divided into five equal parts, such as a sea star

ENDANGERED When the numbers of a species are so low that it may become extinct

EROSION The wearing away of rock or soil by the gradual detachment of fragments by water, wind, and ice

ESTUARY The wide, lower tidal part of a river where it flows into the ocean

EXTINCTION The permanent disappearance of a species, often as a result of hunting or pollution

EXOSKELETON The hard outer case that surrounds an animal's body. It is made of curved plates and tubes that fit together at joints. Crustaceans have an exoskeleton.

FAUNA The animal life found in a particular habitat

FLORA The plant life found growing in a particular habitat

FOSSIL The remains or traces of a living thing preserved in rock

FROND A leaf or leaflike part of a sea plant, sometimes frilled at the edges

FUCOXANTHIN A brown pigment or color in sea plants such as kelp. This pigment masks out chlorophyll, the green pigment present in most plants.

Scarlet ibis, found among coastal fauna of northern South America

GASTROPOD A class of asymmetrical mollusks, including limpets, snails, and slugs, in which the foot is broad and flat and the shell, if any, is in one piece and conical

GRANITE A rough-grained igneous rock that originally formed deep inside the Earth

HABITAT The physical environment or normal abode of a plant or animal

HIGH TIDE The highest point reached on the shore when the tide is in

HOLDFAST A branched structure on a sea plant that attaches itself to a rock and keeps the plant stable in one spot; sometimes also called a hapteron

HOST A living thing that provides food and a home for a parasite

IGNEOUS Any rock solidified from molten material, such as lava.

INTERTIDAL ZONE The area on a beach that lies between the highest and lowest points reached by the tides

INVERTEBRATE An animal that has no backbone

KELP A type of seaweed, often brown and with a holdfast

LAVA Most commonly refers to streams of hot liquid rock that flow from a volcano, but also refers to this rock when it has cooled and solidified

LOW TIDE The lowest point reached on the shore when the tide is out

LUNG A body organ used to breathe air

MIDRIB A central stem in the leaf of a plant

MIGRATION A journey by an animal to a new habitat. Many animals make a regular migration each year to feed or breed.

MINERALS A naturally occurring inorganic substance, which is usually hard. Most rocks are made from minerals.

MUTUALISM A close relationship between two species in which both partners benefit. Clown fish and sea anemones have such a relationship by providing each other with protection from predators.

NEAP TIDE A tide that occurs every 14–15 days and coincides with the first and last quarters of the moon. This tide does not reach very high up or low down the shore.

ORGANISM A living thing

PARASITE An organism that spends part or all of its life in close association with another species, taking food and shelter from it but giving nothing in return

PEDICELLARIA Sharp, beaklike structures that cover the surface of some echinoderms, such as sea urchins. Pedicellaria are used for both feeding and protection.

PHYCOERYTHRIN A red pigment or color in sea plants such as kelp that masks out the green pigment chlorophyll

Plankton with animal and plant components

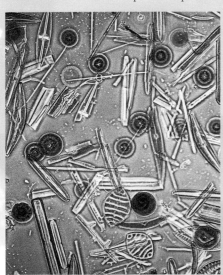

Like all bivalves, mussels are invertebrates.

PLANKTON Minute organisms, including animal and algae, that are found in the surface layers of water. Plankton drift with the current.

POLLUTION Disruption of the natural world by chemicals and other agents

PREDATOR An animal that hunts other animals for food

PREY The animals that are hunted and eaten by a predator

SCAVENGER An animal that feeds on dead plants or animals

SEDIMENT Light rock particles that settle on the ocean floor. Sea water becomes cloudy when this sediment is stirred up

SERRATED A sharply toothed surface, much like a saw

SHALE A type of rock that forms from hardened particles of clay

SILT Tiny particles of rock and mineral that can form the ocean bed

SPECIES A group of living things that can breed together in the wild

SPRING TIDE A tide pattern that occurs every 14–15 days at full and new moons, when the tide reaches the highest up and the lowest down the shore

Clown fish and anemones, mutually beneficial

STIPE The stalk, or stem, of a plant

STRANDLINE The line of washed-up shells, seaweed, driftwood, and other debris left on the beach when the tide has gone out

STRATUM A layer, usually of rock

SYMBIOSIS A close living relationship between two different species that often depend on each other for survival

TEMPERATE A type of climate on Earth, characterized by moderate conditions

TOPSHELL A short cone-shaped shell belonging to a sea-dwelling gastropod

WADER A bird that searches for food on the shoreline, usually by standing in shallow water and probing its long beak into the sand for insects and worms

WRACK One of the main types of seaweed, usually brown in color, and tough and slippery in texture

VEGETATION The plants that grow in a particular habitat

VENOM A poisonous substance in an animal's bite or sting

VERTEBRATE An animal that has a backbone. There are five main groups of vertebrates: fish, amphibians, reptiles, birds, and mammals.

Sea grass is common to coastal vegetation

Index

Acknowledgments

The author and the publisher would like to thank:

Dr. Geoff Potts and the Marine Biological Association of the United Kingdom.
The Booth Museum of Natural History, Brighton, for supplying the specimens on pages 52–55.
Trevor Smith's Animal World.
Collins and Chambers.
Wallace Heaton, Jane Williams, Jonathan Buckley, Barney Kindersley and Dr. David George, Dr. Paul Cornelius, Dr. Bob Symes, David Moore, Ian Tittley, Arthur Chater, Dr. Ray Ingle, Gordon Patterson, Dr. John Taylor, Solene Morris, Susannah van Rose, Alwyne Wheeler, Chris Owen, and Colin Keates of the Natural History Museum.
Richard Czapnik for help with design.
Ella Skene for the index.
Victoria Sorzano for typing.
Fred Ford of Radius Graphics for artwork.
David Burnie for consultancy.

Picture credits
t = top; b = bottom; m = middle; l = left; r = right

Heather Angel: 12br, 23ml, 30tr, 42tl & b, 49br, 69tl
Ardea London Ltd: 54bl
Atlantide SNC/Bruce Coleman Ltd: 67b
Leo Batten/FLPA – Images of Nature: 69c
Erik Bjurstrom/Bruce Coleman Ltd: 70bl
Liz and Tony Bomford/Ardea London Ltd: 66 cr
B Borrell/FLPA: Images of Nature: 66c
Mark Boulton/Bruce Coleman Ltd: 8tl
Professor George Branch: 12b
Jane Burton/Bruce Coleman Ltd.: 45tl
Bob & Clara Calhoun/Bruce Coleman Ltd.: 37m, 43m
N. Callow/NHPA: 31
G.J. Cambridge/NHPA: 15m
Laurie Campbell/NHPA: 24t
James Carmichael Jr./NHPA: 49bl
C. Carvalho/Frank Lane: 23mr
Judith Clarke/Bruce Coleman Ltd.: 71bl
Eric Crichton/Bruce Coleman Ltd.: 20tl
Nicolas Devore/Bruce Coleman Ltd.: 9m
Adrian Evans/Hutchison Library: 10m
Mary Evans Picture Library: 8m, 14tl, 18

& 19b, 20b, 23tr, 26tl, 27, 30tl, 36, 38tl, 47tr, 53tl, 55tl, 56tr & m, 58bl, 59tr
Kenneth W. Fink/Ardea London Ltd: 56bl
Jeff Foott/Bruce Coleman Ltd: 24b, 30ml, 31bl
Neville Fox-Davies/Bruce Coleman Ltd: 25m
J. Frazier/NHPA: 50tr
Pavel German/NHPA: 50tr
Jeff Goodman/NHPA: 40mr & br
Robert Francis/Robert Harding Picture Library: 67tr
Mark E. Gibson/Corbis: 68bl
Francois Gohier/Ardea London Ltd: 69r
Chris Gomersall/Bruce Coleman Ltd: 71tc
P. Guegan/Sunset/FLPA: 67tl
Ian Griffiths/Robert Harding Picture Library: 17br
Tony Hamblin/FLPA: 69bl
Robert Harding Picture Library: 9b, 11bl
Michael Holford/Victoria and Albert Museum: 26br
Scott Johnson/NHPA: 31br, 48m
Tony Jones/Robert Harding: 11tr
M.P. Kahl/Bruce Coleman Ltd: 8bl
Franz Lanting/Bruce Coleman Ltd: 12tl
Richard Matthews/Seaphot Ltd: Planet Earth Pictures: 55m

Marine Biological Association of the United Kingdom: 62tr
John Mitchell/Oxford Scientific Films: 66tl
Mark Newman/FLPA: 67cl
M. Nimmo/Frank Lane: 8tr
Fritz Polking GDT/Frank Lane: 44m, 64tr
Dr. Geoff Potts: 30b
Mike Price/SAL/Oxford Scientific Films: 65br
Niall Rankin/Eric Hosking: 54br
Joel W. Rogers/Corbis: 66b
Walter Rohdich/FLPA: 65t
Ann Ronan Picture Library: 8br
John Taylor/Bruce Coleman Ltd: 43br
Kim Taylor/Bruce Coleman Ltd: 39tr
Roger Tidman/Frank Lane: 10tr
M.I. Walker/NHPA: 71bl
W. Wisniewski/FLPA: 67
Norbert Wu/NHPA: 64b
Bill Wood/NHPA: 40ml
Gunter Ziesler/Bruce Coleman Ltd: 29b
Jacket credits: Front: Densey Clyne Productions/OSF, b.
All other images © Dorling Kindersley.
For further information see:
www.dkimages.com
Illustrations by: John Woodcock
Picture research by: Elizabeth Eyres